COME SIGN WITH US

Sign Language Activities for Children

Second Edition

Jan C. Hafer
Robert M. Wilson

Illustrations by Paul Setzer

CLERC BOOKS

Gallaudet University Press
Washington, D.C.

Photographs by Richard T. Nowitz.
Cover design by Auras Designs, Washington, D.C.

The signs in this book may be reproduced for classroom use only.

Clerc Books
An imprint of Gallaudet University Press
Washington, DC 20002

05 04 03 02 01 00 99 98 97 96 5 4 3 2 1

Library of Congress Cataloging-in-Publication Data

Hafer, Jan Christian.
    Come sign with us: sign language activities for children / Jan C.
Hafer, Robert M. Wilson ; illustrations by Paul Setzer. — 2nd ed.
        p.   cm.
    "Clerc books."
    Includes bibliographical references.
    ISBN 1–56368–051–3 (alk. paper)
    1. Sign language—Study and teaching (Elementary)—Activity
programs.   2. American Sign Language—Study and teaching
(Elementary)—Activity programs.   I. Wilson, Robert Mills.
    II. Setzer, Paul M.   III. Title.
HV2474.H32   1996
371.91 '27—dc20   96–24798
                                                      CIP

CONTENTS

INTRODUCTION

Congratulations

You are about to begin a very exciting series of lessons with your students. Together, you will enter a new world of communication. Besides learning a different way of "talking," your students may also discover that they remember the meaning of many spoken English words better when they also learn to sign the words.

After completing these lessons, you and your students will be able to converse with Deaf people. As you interact more with people who are deaf, your signing skills will inevitably improve. Today, hearing and deaf children often attend school together. Ample opportunities exist for hearing children to practice their signing skills with deaf friends. You can set the stage for comfortable communication by providing instruction in sign language, by involving deaf children (and adults, whenever possible) in that instruction, and by demonstrating an accepting and respectful attitude of language differences among people.

WHAT IS SIGN LANGUAGE?

To define sign language, let us first consider American Sign Language, or ASL, as it is often called. ASL is the primary, or "native," language used by the Deaf community in the United States. It is a visual-gestural language, unlike spoken English, which is auditory-vocal. The grammatical rules of ASL differ from those of spoken English. The signs in ASL sentences are put together in a different order than words are put together in English sentences. For example, to convey the same meaning as "I haven't eaten yet," you would silently sign NOT YET EAT ME with appropriate facial expression. Anyone interested in learning the language should become familiar with the linguistics of ASL. This book will provide only a very brief introduction to the subject. (For more detailed information see the references on ASL in the Annotated

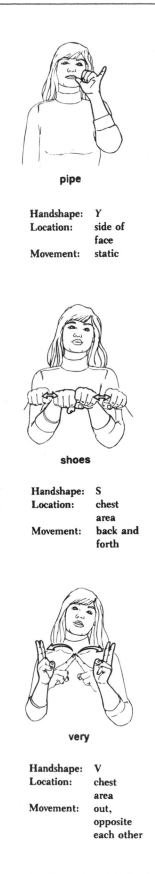

pipe

Handshape: Y
Location: side of
face
Movement: static

shoes

Handshape: S
Location: chest
area
Movement: back and
forth

very

Handshape: V
Location: chest
area
Movement: out,
opposite
each other

Figure 1. Examples of distinctive features in ASL.

Bibliography beginning on page 120.) It is important to remember that ASL is the preferred language of the Deaf community. However, Deaf people do use other forms of signing depending on the situation they find themselves in.

Often when Deaf and hearing people communicate, they use the vocabulary of ASL, but they put the signs in English word order. This form of sign language is called Pidgin Sign English (PSE), or contact signing, and it enables both Deaf and hearing people to speak and sign at the same time, if they choose. ASL has been adapted in other ways to more closely represent English. These adaptations are really communication systems, not languages. In this book, PSE will be used. Our goal is to bring hearing children in public schools who are beginning to learn sign language together with children who are deaf, who may be fluent in sign or who are also just beginning to learn to sign.

Your students must become aware that sign language is a living language. Deaf people use it every day to argue, joke, declare love, or express sorrow. It is this vital, beautiful language that binds the Deaf community together and ensures its existence.

The Features of American Sign Language

Like spoken words, signs can be broken down into specific parts or distinctive features. Linguists who have studied sign language have found that individual signs have three features: *handshape*—how the hand is formed, *location*—where that handshape is placed, and *movement*—where and how the handshape moves (see figure 1).

Most of the handshapes used to create signs come from the letters of the manual alphabet and the manual numbers 1, 2, 3, 4, 5, 9, and 10; or a slight modification of these letters or numbers. Figures 2 and 3 illustrate the manual alphabet and numbers. Figure 4 illustrates some of the modified handshapes found in sign language.

Almost all signs are made in an area around the signer called the *sign space*. This enables the receiver (person watching the signer) to view the signer's face and hands at the same time (see figure 5).

Another important component of sign language is *facial expression*. The face reveals shades of meaning at the same time the hands are "talking." So it is important to have the appropriate facial expression for the message you are trying to convey. Linguists have discovered that there are rules that govern the use of facial expression in sign languages. Figure 6 includes some examples of facial expressions and signs.

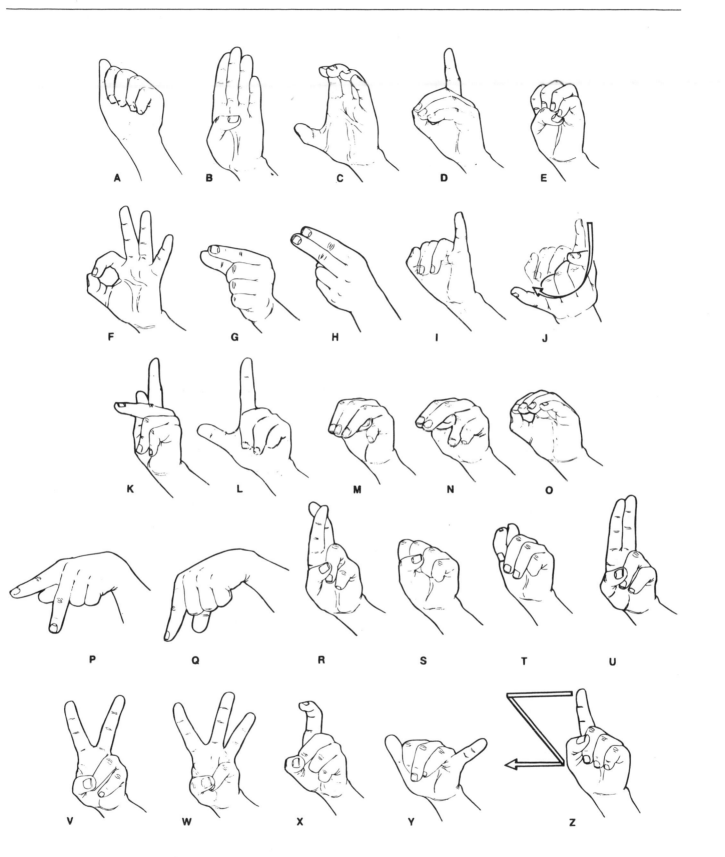

Figure 2.   The American manual alphabet.

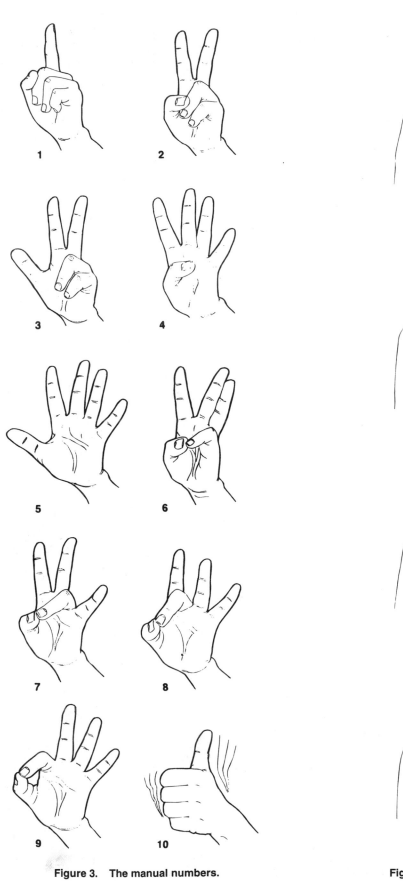

Figure 3.   The manual numbers.

open B

bent V

claw

flat O

Figure 4.   Modified handshapes.

Tips for Learning Signs

As with learning any new skill, commitment and perseverance are important!

Figure 5.   Sign space.

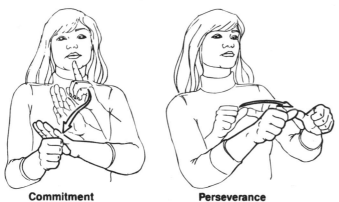

Commitment   Perseverance

However, you can take steps to ensure that you and your students are signing accurately. First, double-check yourself. When you attempt to make a sign from this book, recheck the handshape, the direction of the arrows, and the facial erpression. You should also read the sign descriptions in the glossary to help you make the signs correctly. Practice double-checking with the sign for the word *thrilling*. Don't expect to make the sign perfectly the first time!

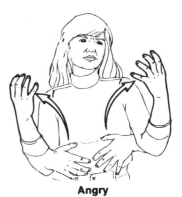

Angry

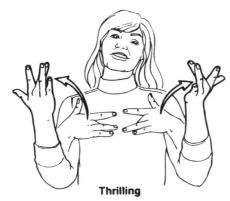

Thrilling

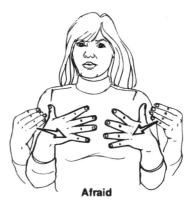

Afraid

Signing is fun to learn and fun to teach. Along with the fun, however, comes some responsibility. The responsibility to teach signs accurately is foremost. Whenever possible, find a Deaf person or a hearing person who is skilled in sign language to be your *sign monitor*. The sign monitor can help you understand what you are learning from using this book. He or she can also help you develop and refine your signing skill by teaching you additional vocabulary and helping you to clearly communicate in a visual language. You can also view the companion videotape, "Come Sign With Us," with your class to see how real kids learn to sign.

HISTORICAL PERSPECTIVES

The American Deaf community has been bound together by sign language for more than 200 years. Deaf people themselves created

What

Figure 6.   The relationship between signs and facial expression.

sign language out of the innate need to communicate that all humans seem to have. American Sign Language (ASL) has its roots in French Sign Language even though our spoken language is English. The history of ASL is related to the history of deaf education in America.

In 1815 Thomas Hopkins Gallaudet, a young seminarian, met a little deaf girl named Alice Cogswell. Dr. Mason Cogswell, Alice's father, persuaded Gallaudet to try to teach his daughter. Gallaudet had some success, but realized he needed more training. At that time in the United States there were no schools for the deaf, so Gallaudet decided to go abroad to study. First, he went to England to study at the Braidwood school, a school that advocated the oral approach to educating deaf children.

Gallaudet

The Braidwood family was very secretive about its teaching methods. They planned to open a school in the United States, so they did not cooperate with Gallaudet. While in London, Gallaudet attended a lecture on the French method of teaching deaf children. He decided to go to Paris and study with the Abbé Roch Ambroise Sicard, the head of the school for the deaf in Paris.

Abbé Sicard's method of teaching deaf children was based on Old French Sign Language, the language used by the Deaf community in Paris. Sicard then added signs to represent the grammatical structures of spoken and written French. Gallaudet learned this "new" signed language (linguists refer to this as Old Signed French) as well as the teaching methods used at the school. When he was ready to return to the United States, Gallaudet persuaded a teacher at the school, a deaf man named Laurent Clerc, to come with him to establish a school for deaf children. Clerc agreed.

Clerc

In 1817 the Connecticut Asylum For the Education and Instruction of Deaf and Dumb Persons was established in Hartford, Connecticut. This school is known today as the American School for the Deaf, and it is the oldest school for the deaf in the United States. Clerc and Gallaudet introduced French Sign Language to their students, who were communicating with their own sign language. This blending of signs became American Sign Language.

Sign Language and the Education of Deaf Children

The use of sign language to teach deaf children has had a long and controversial history. The approach used at the American School for the Deaf included signs as well as speech and speechreading (lipreading). This was called the combined method. In the early years of deaf education in the United States, schools used either the manual method (meaning they only signed in class) or the combined method. Later in the nineteenth century, the Clarke School for the

Deaf in Massachusetts introduced the purely oral approach and prohibited the use of sign language in the school. By the end of the century, these two approaches to the education of deaf children had generated considerable controversy and no agreement between their respective advocates. With improved hearing aid technology, the twentieth century saw an increased emphasis on the use of amplification, speech training, and speechreading. Most schools for the deaf used the oral approach to teach young Deaf children, but allowed the use of signs at the high-school level. The oral approach reigned in deaf education until the 1960s.

Studies done in the 1960s (Donald F. Moores, *Educating the Deaf: Psychology, Principles and Practices* [Houghton Mifflin, 1978], 290–294) showed that deaf children were graduating from high school with less than a sixth-grade reading level. Studies also found that Deaf children of Deaf parents had much higher achievement levels than deaf children of hearing parents. Researchers attributed this to the fact that Deaf parents signed to their Deaf children from infancy while hearing parents, for the most part, did not. Early exposure to signing gives Deaf children clear access to language—a skill essential for success in school. The conclusions reached by researchers led to a new open attitude toward the use of sign language in education, from which the philosophy of Total Communication was born.

Deaf

Total Communication revolutionized the education of deaf children. The basis of this philosophy, simply stated, is that deaf children have a right to use whatever communication mode they need to communicate—gestures, sign language, speech, speechreading, amplification, etc. No restrictions are placed on communication, and sign language is respected and valued as an integral part of educating deaf children. Today, more than 70 percent of the educational programs for deaf children in the United States employ the philosophy of Total Communication.

Sign

A new approach to education of children who are Deaf has emerged in recent years. This Bilingual/Bicultural (Bi-Bi) approach recognizes the distinction between spoken and written English and American Sign Language. The two languages are used separately, not simultaneously communicated (that is, no speaking and signing at the same time). Proponents of this approach consider ASL the native language of Deaf children and believe competency in ASL precedes English competency. However, both languages are valued equally.

SIGNING FOR HEARING POPULATIONS

All deaf children in public school settings are now mainstreamed for portions of their school day. It is important for hearing children to be able to sign in order to facilitate communication with these deaf children. Formal instruction in signing is important so that the signs are made properly and clearly. It is our observation that hearing children take great pride in their newly learned signing skills and are anxious to use them.

Sign language seems to be popular among other hearing groups as well. The April 21, 1988 edition of the *New York Times* carried an article by Edwin McDowell entitled, "Books for Deaf Find a Wider Market." In that article, McDowell discussed the interest in signing shown by bookstores, book clubs, and professional groups such as lawyers and medical and law enforcement personnel. Many programs for special needs students (e.g., mentally handicapped, language-delayed, and speech-impaired children; and speakers of English as a second language) use sign language as a way to improve students' language skills. Books, sheet music, nursery rhymes, plays, videotapes, charts, workbooks, and pamphlets are available to assist these programs.

Some hearing educators also use sign language to help their students learn sight vocabulary for reading. Children who seem to learn their sight vocabulary one day, but forget it the next, profit greatly from signing instruction. Learning-disabled children also learn sight words easily through signing. Even adult illiterates have found signing to be an effective way to learn sight vocabulary.

Signing has gained such great respect, that many universities now include sign language as one of the languages offered to fulfill foreign language requirements. Sign language is the fourth most common language used in the United States, after English, Spanish, and Italian. It seems natural, then, for signing to be taught to all children in a systematic manner. That, of course, is the purpose of this book.

USING THIS BOOK

The following twenty lessons have been developed to help you teach beginning sign language. The objective of each lesson is to introduce the target vocabulary in a format that is both familiar and interesting to children. The target vocabulary is presented in English and Spanish because many teachers now have students whose first language is Spanish. The signs for the target vocabulary in this book are from American Sign Language. We believe that the addition of the Spanish words will make the book appealing to Spanish-speaking children and their teachers. It will also provide students with an additional opportunity to become aware of yet another language used by many people who live in the United States.

General Lesson Plan Format

The lesson plans on the following pages focus on various topics of interest to children. Each lesson plan includes

1.   Topic Sentence—The topic sentence can be used by the teacher to introduce the lesson. The signs for the topic sentence are arranged above the sentence. These signs may be taught to the students along with the target vocabulary. The model signing the topic sentences is left-handed. Right-handed signers should reverse the hand positions shown.

2.   Target Vocabulary—The target vocabulary introduces approximately ten signs. Each sign is identified by its English and Spanish equivalent. At the end of the lesson, children should be able to use the signs expressively and receptively; that is, they should be able to make the signs when they need to and they should be able to understand the signs when they are made by others. Teachers should photocopy the signs so that students can make their own sign language books.

3.   Note to the Teacher—The note to the teacher contains background information related to the lesson.

4.   The Lesson—The lesson contains step-by-step instructions for teaching the target vocabulary. The objectives for each lesson are
   a. to enrich the child's vocabulary;
   b. to provide an enjoyable and an exciting learning experience. Any fear of signing should be quickly overcome.
   c. to make the children comfortable with signs so that they can use them to communicate with deaf people when they have the opportunity.

5.   Context Activity—Suggestions are provided for reinforcing the use of signs in context (sentences). Some lessons have the context built into the lesson.

6.   Follow-up Activities—These are activities the teacher can do as a follow-up to the lessons in each section.

7.   Notes—Space is provided for the teacher to record additional teaching strategies or information (new books, resource people, etc.) that may be helpful in the teaching process.

Though each lesson includes step-by-step procedures, the following strategies are not repeated in each lesson. These are general procedures that all teachers use in every lesson.

1.   Develop anticipatory set
2.   Communicate the objectives
3.   Provide guided practice
4.   Check for understanding
5.   Provide for independent practice
6.   Provide closure to the lesson.

SUGGESTED LESSON PLANS

There are many approaches to teaching sign language. We have incorporated lesson-format suggestions that are familiar to most elementary school teachers. Using these formats will help you incorporate sign instruction into your language arts program more easily. This approach is especially helpful for teachers who are not fluent in ASL but who wish to introduce signing in their classrooms. The teaching of the sign vocabulary is naturally a part of the language arts block.

We encourage teachers to experiment with different ways to teach sign vocabulary and conversational skills to their students. A flexible and individual approach is best.

The following six lesson-format suggestions are included to help you generate enthusiam among your students for learning signs. Each format suggestion contains an example from one of the actual lessons in the book; however, each format suggestion is usable with any lesson in the book.

SUGGESTION ONE: SEMANTIC CATEGORIES

1. Teacher lists three known words.
2. Teacher lists one new word.
3. Teacher leaves space for children to add words that fit the category.

Example: From Lesson 13

Holidays
Thanksgiving
Christmas   } known words
Fourth of July

Hanukkah   }   new word

_____

_____

Teacher picks the new word, *Hanukkah*, and introduces it through known words in the same semantic category. Children can add new words as they learn them.

Source: J. P. Gipe, "Use of Relevant Context Helps Kids Learn New Word Meanings," *The Reading Teacher*, 33 (1980): 398–402.

SUGGESTION TWO: VOCABULARY GRID

The teacher prepares a grid and explains to the children that they should place a check mark under the appropriate categories.

Example: From Lesson 15

	ANIMAL CATEGORIES					
Animals	Pets	Zoo	Farm	Large	Small	Strong
Horse			✔	✔		✔
Cat	✔				✔	
Lion		✔		✔		✔
Bull						
Elephant						
Dog						
Rabbit						
Panda						
Sheep						
Cow						
Monkey						

This activity helps students think about relationships of new words and their prior knowledge. Animals may fit more than one category and, in some cases, children might not agree. For example, is a panda large or small?

Source: P. L. Anders and C. S. Bos, "Semantic Feature Analysis: An Interactive Strategy for Vocabulary Development and Text Comprehension," *Journal of Reading*, 29 (1986): 610–616.

SUGGESTION THREE: WORD MAPS

The teacher writes a series of questions, places a new word in the center, and helps the children identify answers to the questions.

Example: From Lesson 15

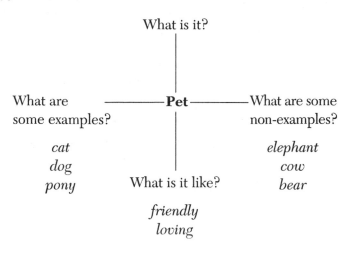

This activity helps children internalize new words beyond the level of definition.

Source: R. M. Schwartz and T. E. Raphael, "Concepts of Definitions: A Key to Improving Students' Vocabulary," *The Reading Teacher*, 39 (1985):198–205.

SUGGESTION FOUR: WEBBING

Webs can take many forms. This one is a topic web and can be used to graphically illustrate word opposites.

Example: From Lesson 9

1. Teacher places topic in the center of the web.

   Opposites

2. Teacher and/or children place word-opposite pairs around the center. These can be signs of opposites, the opposites in word form, or both.

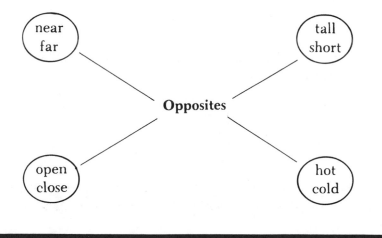

This activity assists children with the organization of ideas through graphic display. It is excellent preparation for retelling stories or writing. Webs also make interesting bulletin boards.

Source: F. Lyman, C. Lopez, and A. Mindus, *Language Arts Guide.* (Clarksville, MD: Howard County Board of Education, 1977).

SUGGESTION FIVE: PERSONAL OUTLINING

After reading a selection, the teacher asks children to contribute what they think was most interesting or most important. These ideas are recorded on the board or on chart paper.

Example: From Lesson 20

After everyone has had a chance to contribute, the teacher then either models on the board or chart paper or has handouts that look like the following:

1. Signing is important. _____
   important idea
   a. Deaf people need sign language to communicate with each other. _____
      supporting detail
   b. Deaf and hearing people need sign language to communicate with each other. _____
      supporting detail
   c. _____
      supporting detail
2. Signing is fun. _____
   important idea
   a. Children enjoy learning signs. _____
      supporting detail

Children are to pick from the list of interesting or important ideas and place it on line 1. and then either recall or reread to find supporting details. The second interesting or important idea can be placed on line 2., etc., etc. The teacher can now teach the signs for these important ideas and supporting details.

This activity helps children understand important ideas and details. It is an excellent preparation for written or oral reporting.

Source: R. Wilson and C. Cleland. *Diagnostic and Remedial Reading.* (Columbus, OH: Merrill, 1989): 276–277.

SUGGESTION SIX: SEQUENCE BAR OR CIRCLE

Sequence bars help children understand the nature of sequences. The teacher draws a large bar on the board or on chart paper.

Example: From Lesson 12

The sign for each day can be drawn in each day's column. The children are instructed to draw a picture of something they did on each of these days. Below the picture they can write a short phrase or sentence about their activity.

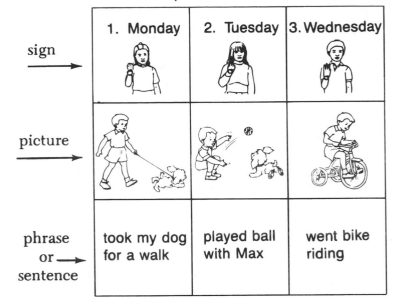

Sequence bars make nice room decorations and serve as a reminder to the children that days happen in sequence.

This type of activity can be used for story sequences using circle stories, as the following example illustrates.

Circle Story

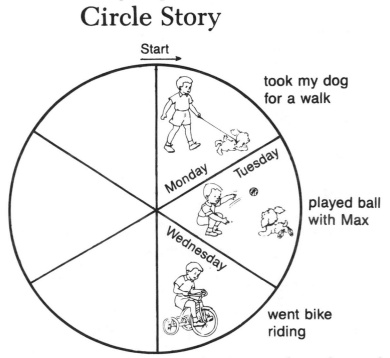

Source: J. A. Vogel. "Story Circles Teach Sequence," *The Reading Teacher,* 41 (1987): 250–251.

1

FACIAL EXPRESSIONS

In this lesson, work on the expressions for *happy, sad, mad, puzzled, afraid,* **and** *surprised.*

NOTE TO THE TEACHER

Facial expressions show how you feel. As you have already read, facial expressions are an integral part of sign language. This aspect is a logical choice for beginning instruction in sign. This lesson is nonverbal and nonmanual. The possibilities are endless for introducing children to the range of feelings that are expressed through changes in our faces. This lesson will lay a foundation for clear communication in sign as well as spoken communication.

THE LESSON

Tell the children that today they will be allowed to make faces! Encourage a discussion about what is meant by "making faces," asking students to explain and give examples. Ask students to share previous experiences when they made faces at someone and did not use words.

Explain to the students that making faces helps people communicate clearly. Set the mood by telling the children about something that makes you very happy. As you share this with the class, smile. It is easy to do because it is natural. Then, ask the children to think of something that makes them happy. Walk around the room with a mirror saying "Mirror, mirror, in my hand, who's the *happiest* in the land?" Hand the mirror to one child

at a time and have each one look at his or her expression in the mirror. Ask each child to share the happy thought and demonstrate the facial expression to the class. Give other students an opportunity, too.

Move on to the next facial expression. After all the facial expressions have been demonstrated, ask for volunteers to come forward to review them with the class. Have the class ask the volunteers to demonstrate each facial expression as the class guesses.

Tell the class that you will be practicing the facial expressions throughout the rest of the day and that they must be ready! As the day progresses, make a statement, such as, "It's time for recess, how do you feel?" The children should respond with a facial expression, not a spoken word. Remind the children that they will be using these facial expressions as they learn to sign. Suggest that the children share this activity with their families.

FOLLOW-UP ACTIVITY

Create a bulletin board display with photos of your students demonstrating various facial expressions. Have them write a sentence about each facial expression under each photo. As they learn the signs for feelings related to the facial expressions, such as "happy", "sad", "angry", etc., add the corresponding illustrations from this book, or take additional photos of the children signing the vocabulary.

NOTES

2

LEARNING TO SEE SIGNS

NOTE TO THE TEACHER

Train your eyes to see signs. As you teach sign language you will become aware of how important it is to train the children's eyes to "see" signs. The following lesson will help children begin to use their eyes in a different way. This lesson is a variation on an activity developed by Gilbert Eastman of the Gallaudet University Drama Department. The activity is called "change-the-stick."

THE LESSON

Arrange the children in a circle. You may want to divide your class into groups of five or six. Begin by telling the children that you have a "magic" (imaginary) stick that can change into lots of different things. Pick up the "magic" stick and mime a stick-like object, such as a fishing pole, a flag, a baton, a baseball bat, etc. Explain each object and help the children see the mime action as an outline of the real object. Pass the object on to a student. Encourage the student to imitate your action for each object. After each student has a turn demonstrating the object, ask the students to demonstrate all of the objects that were presented. If students seem to have difficulty, use pictures to prompt the creative process. Tell the children that the "eye exercise" they just participated in will help them learn sign language.

FOLLOW-UP ACTIVITY

Make a list of familiar verbs. Conduct a similar lesson acting out the verbs. As you learn the signs for the verbs, compare the action of the mimed verb with the actual sign.

NOTES

FINGERSPELLING

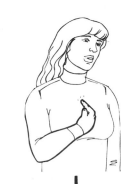

I   **want**   **to spell**

words   **with**   **my**   **hand.**

NOTE TO THE TEACHER

Children should already know their ABC's for this lesson. If they don't, you may want to use the manual alphabet letter to reinforce the learning of the printed letter as each one is presented in class. In preparation for teaching the manual alphabet, explain to the students that spelling words on the hand is called fingerspelling. *You can fingerspell a word anytime you don't know the sign for it. When you fingerspell, keep these guidelines in mind.*

1. Fingerspell with the hand you write with. If you are left-handed, then fingerspell with your left hand.
2. Always fingerspell with the palm of your hand facing the person with whom you are communicating, except for the letters G, and H.

G   **H**

3. *Try* to say the word (either out loud or in your head) as you fingerspell it—do not say the individual letters. This helps you think of the *whole word.*

When you demonstrate the manual alphabet, stress the similarity of some of the letters to their printed counterparts.

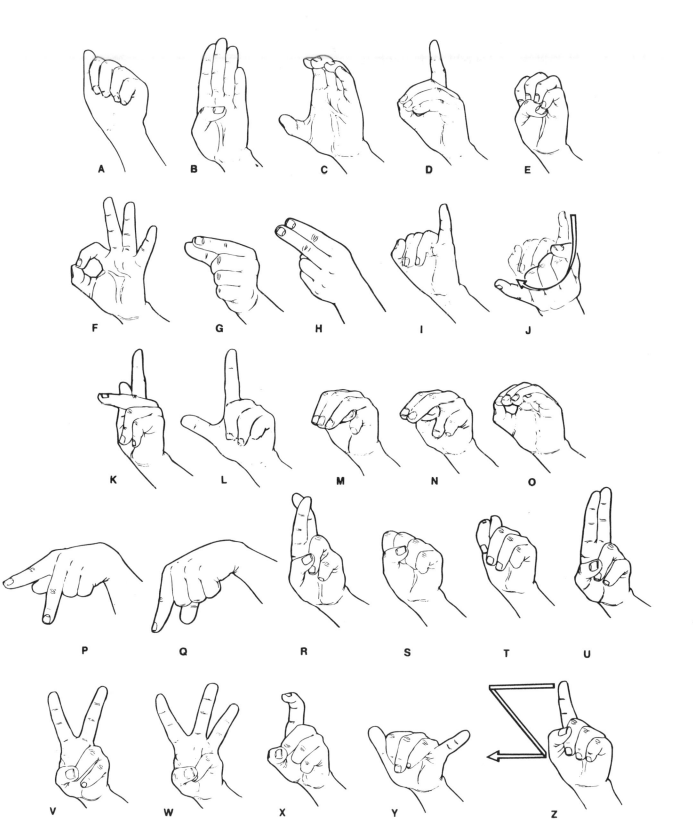

American Manual Alphabet

THE LESSON

Begin teaching the alphabet by five letters a day. Model each letter and have the children imitate. Have the students practice in small groups or pairs, and encourage them to mix up the letters as they practice (for example, *b-d-a-c*). Monitor the practice and correct any incorrect fingerspelling.

As soon as the children have learned to fingerspell the alphabet, have them spell words that they already know (for example, *c-a-t, b-o-y, g-i-r-l, l-u-n-c-h*). Also, let the children fingerspell their names throughout the day.

Once learned, fingerspelling should be practiced every day. Say the sentence, "Now we will have *r-e-a-d-i-n-g*," or "It's time for *l-u-n-c-h*," and fingerspell the key word. As the children see the fingerspelling have them imitate it. Be sure to distribute the handout for fingerspelling as you teach them the letters.

Fingerspelling can be used to reinforce a number of skills in the classroom. You will find it effortless to add a new dimension to learning such skills as spelling, phonics, and alphabetizing. Remember that fingerspelling adds a multisensory component to learning, which is so important to young children.

FOLLOW-UP ACTIVITY

Conduct a spelling test a different way! Fingerspell the words to the class and have them write the words. You can also have individual spelling sessions with the students where they fingerspell selected words to you.

NOTES

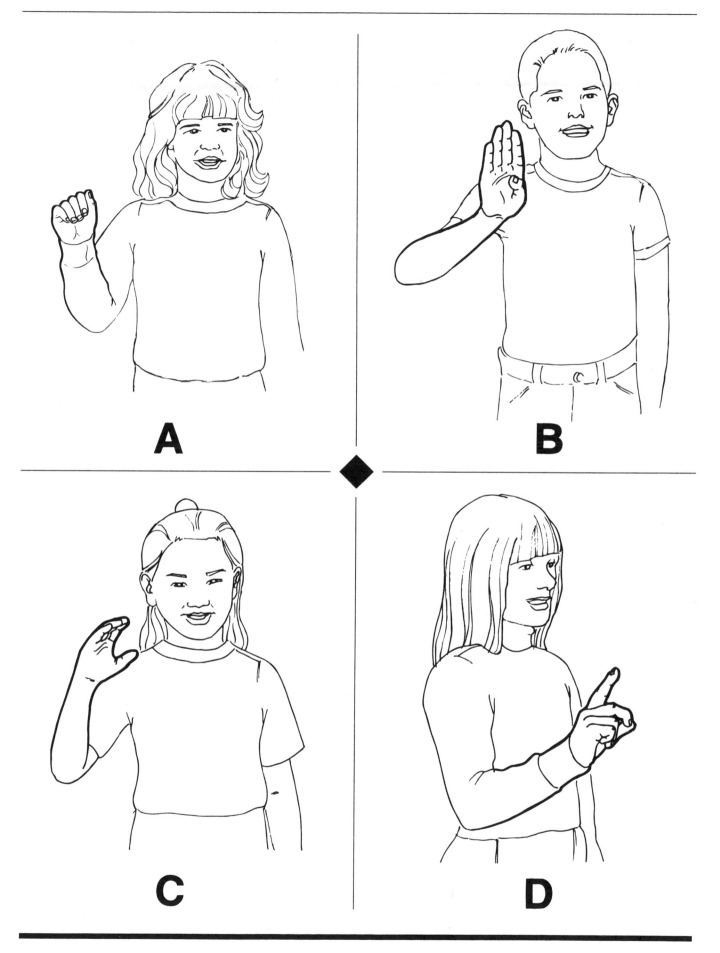

A

B

C

D

E

F

G

H

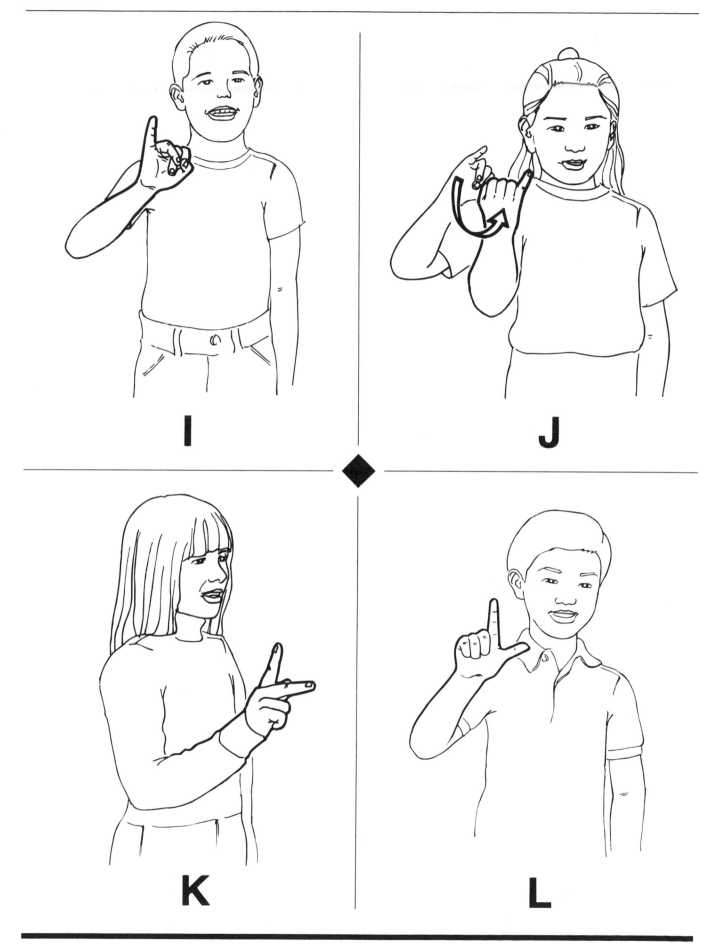

I

J

K

L

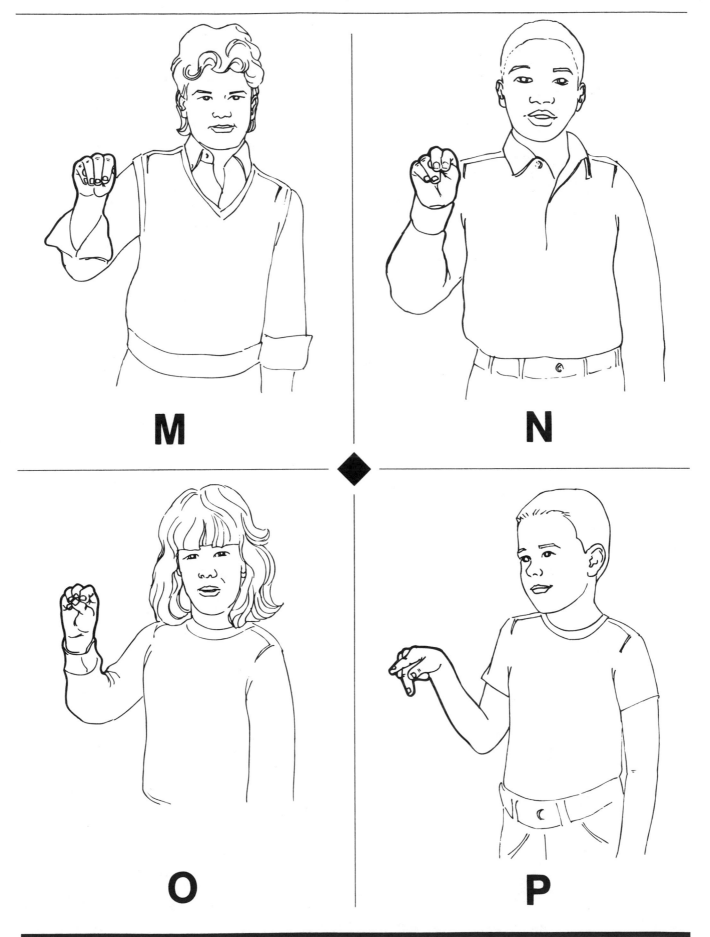

M

N

O

P

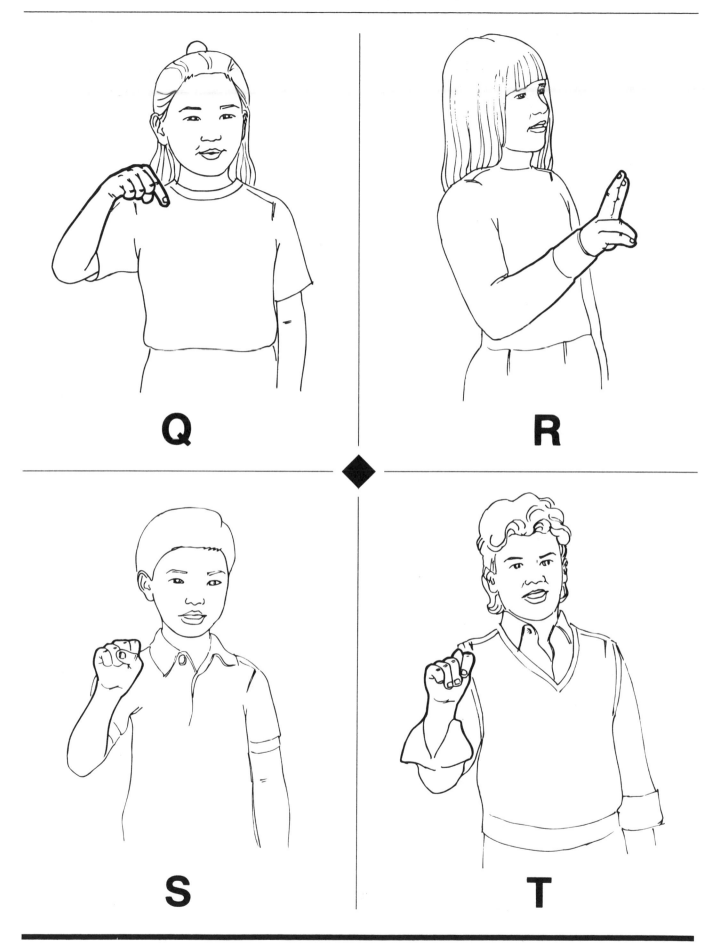

Q

R

S

T

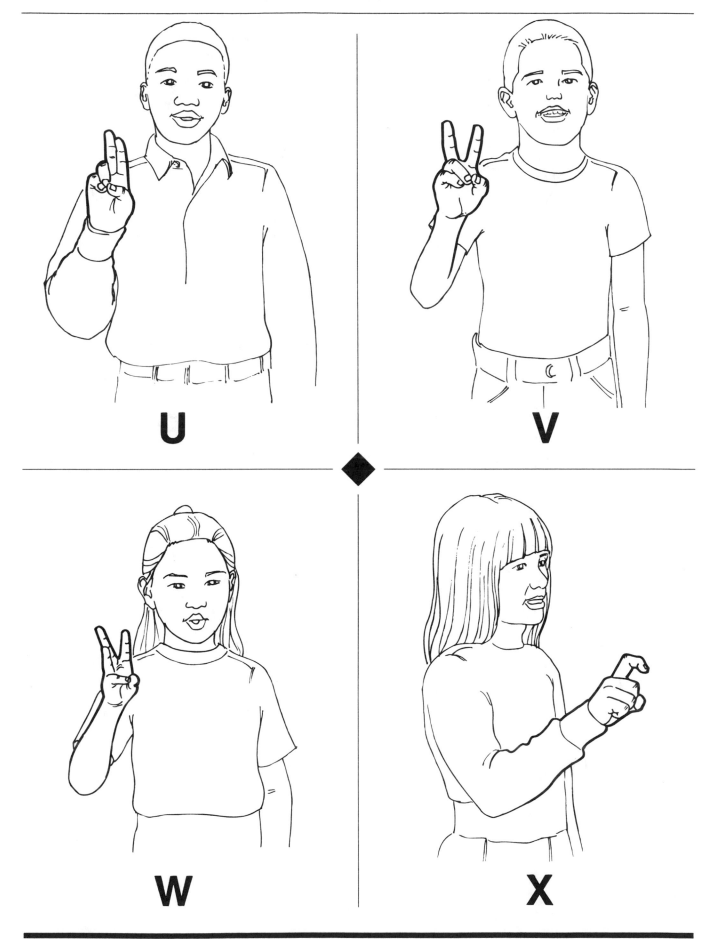

U

V

W

X

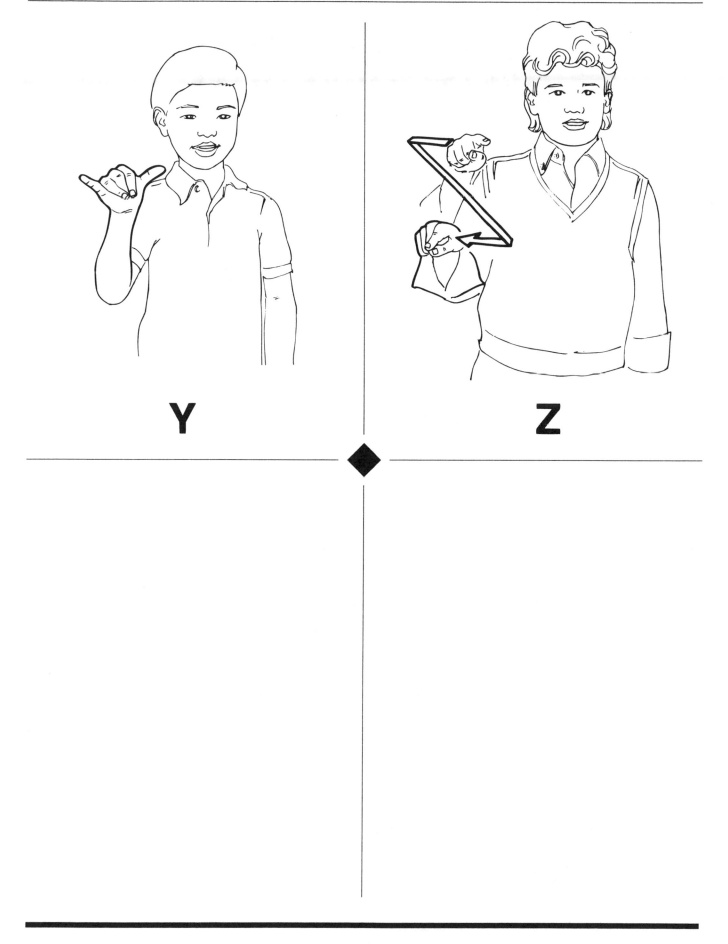

Y

Z

4
ASKING QUESTIONS

Do   **you**   **have**

any   **questions?**

TARGET VOCABULARY

English/*Spanish*

what?	why?	What's up?
¿qué?	*¿por qué?*	*¿Qué pasa?*
where?	do	What are you doing?
¿dónde?	*hacer*	*¿Qué estás haciendo?*
when?	can	
¿cuándo?	*poder*	
who?	how?	
¿quién?	*¿cómo?*	

NOTE TO THE TEACHER

This lesson on question words is presented after the fingerspelling lesson so that your students will be able to make sentences immediately. After they learn to sign the question words, they can fingerspell the rest of what they want to say, or they can just say the rest of the words in the sentence if they are unable to fingerspell the words.

THE LESSON

Start the lesson with a discussion about new vocabulary. Have the students give you sentences using each of the question words selected for this lesson (for example, What is your name? Why are you learning signs?). They should then write their sentences on the chalkboard or on chart paper. The students can take turns signing and fingerspelling each other's sentences. You should model the signs as the children attempt them and then serve as the sign monitor until the children sign the words correctly.

The signs for *What's up?* and *What are you doing?* are ASL signs. Often in ASL, one sign signed in a particular way can mean a whole sentence. *What's up?* and *What are you doing?* are two examples. They are fun to sign! When you teach these signs, tell the students they don't have to sign every word in the phrase, but just one special sign. Ask a deaf friend or a hearing person skilled in signing (your sign monitor) to show the class more examples of this feature of ASL.

CONTEXT ACTIVITY

Have the children read your signs in the following sentences:

Where are my shoes?
What is your name?
How old are you?
Why are you mad?

FOLLOW-UP ACTIVITY

Immediately following this lesson, sign the question words each time you use them during the rest of the day.

NOTES

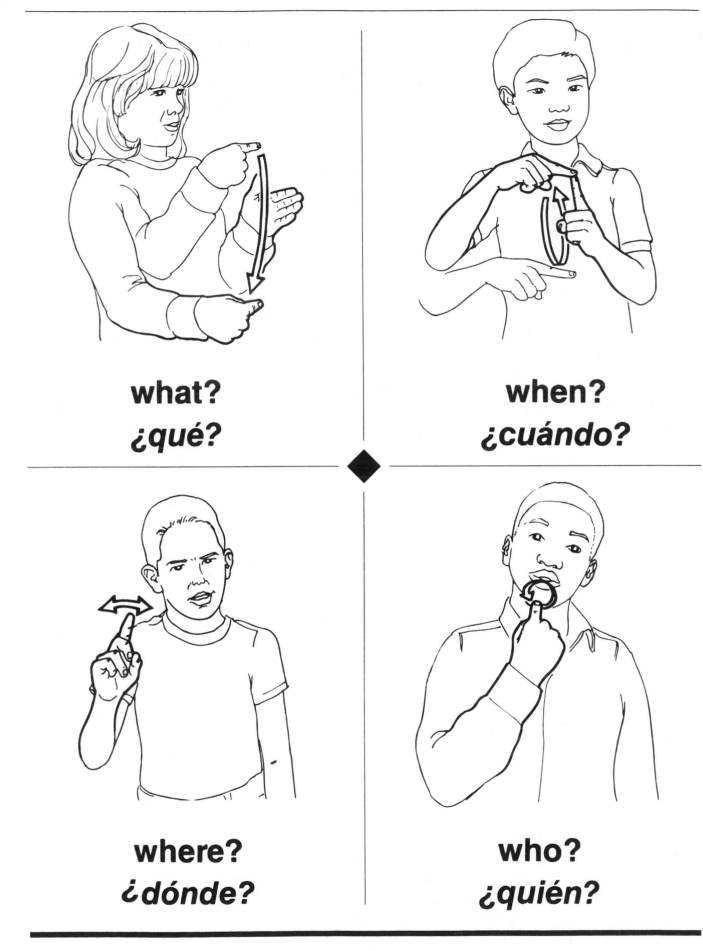

what?
¿qué?

when?
¿cuándo?

where?
¿dónde?

who?
¿quién?

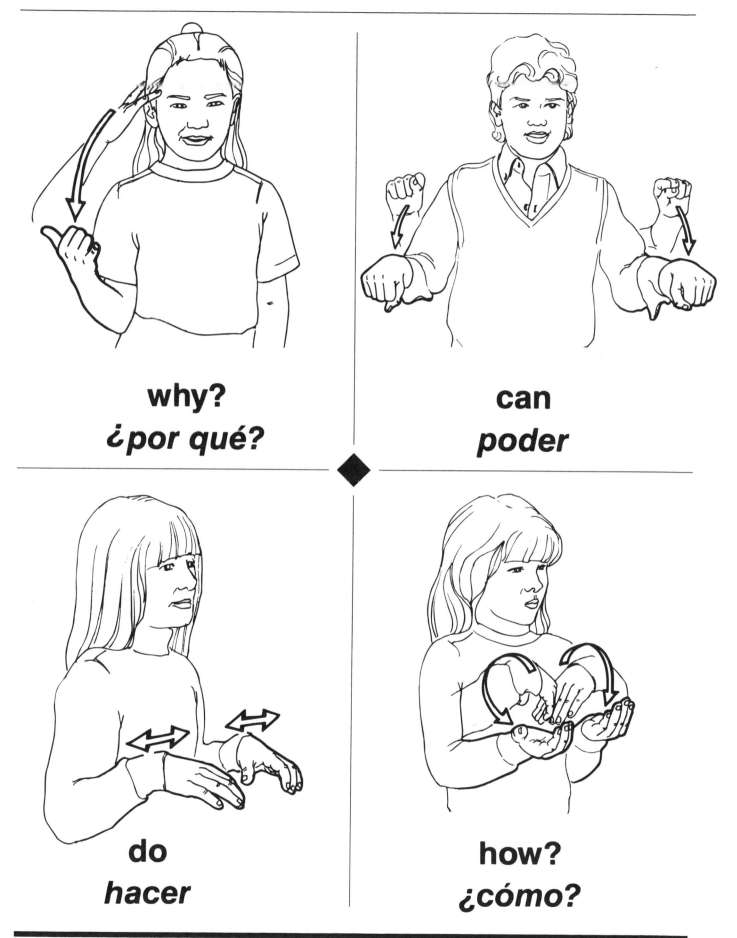

why?
¿por qué?

can
poder

do
hacer

how?
¿cómo?

What's up?
¿Qué pasa?

What are you doing?
¿Qué estás haciendo?

SAYING HELLO

  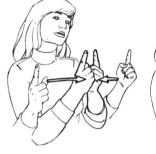 

We **will** **meet** **some**

 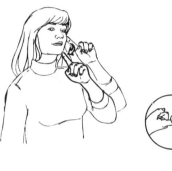 

new **deaf** **friends.**

TARGET VOCABULARY

English/*Spanish*

hello	go	live	friend
hola	*ir*	*vivir*	*amigo*
my	your	want	fine
mi	*tu*	*querer*	*bien*
name	old	school	
nombre	*viejo/años*	*escuela*	

NOTE TO THE TEACHER

When combined with the question words and fingerspelling, your students will be able to sign a lot of sentences after they complete this lesson.

THE LESSON

Ask the students what they would do if they met a deaf child on the playground or at the park. Discuss their ideas. They will probably say that they would fingerspell. Ask them if they would like to learn the signs for making new friends. We guarantee they will say yes! Ask them what kinds of things they would say to someone they just met. You may want to write these ideas on the board. Taking the student-generated ideas, introduce the sign vocabulary to your class. Encourage students to fingerspell words they don't know how to sign. At this point, the students will be fingerspelling their names.

You may want to include the following sample sentences in this lesson. You can sign the bold words.

> **Hello**, how are you?
> *Ola, ¿cómo estás?*

> **Fine**, how are you?
> *Bien, ¿y tu?*

> What's your **name**?
> *¿Cómo te llamas?*

How **old** are you?
¿Cuántos años tienes?

Where do you go to **school**?
¿A qué escuela vas?

Where do you **live**?
¿A dónde vives?

Do you want to be my **friend**?
¿Quieres ser mi amigo?

FOLLOW-UP ACTIVITY

As a group, write a short skit about meeting people. Incorporate the sign vocabulary you have just learned. Have the students practice signing the skit. Videotape and view it with the class so they can see what they look like as they sign. Discuss the accuracy and clarity of their signing and fingerspelling. Ask the group for ideas on how the entire class can improve their signing skills.

NOTES

hello
hola

name
nombre

my
mi

go
ir

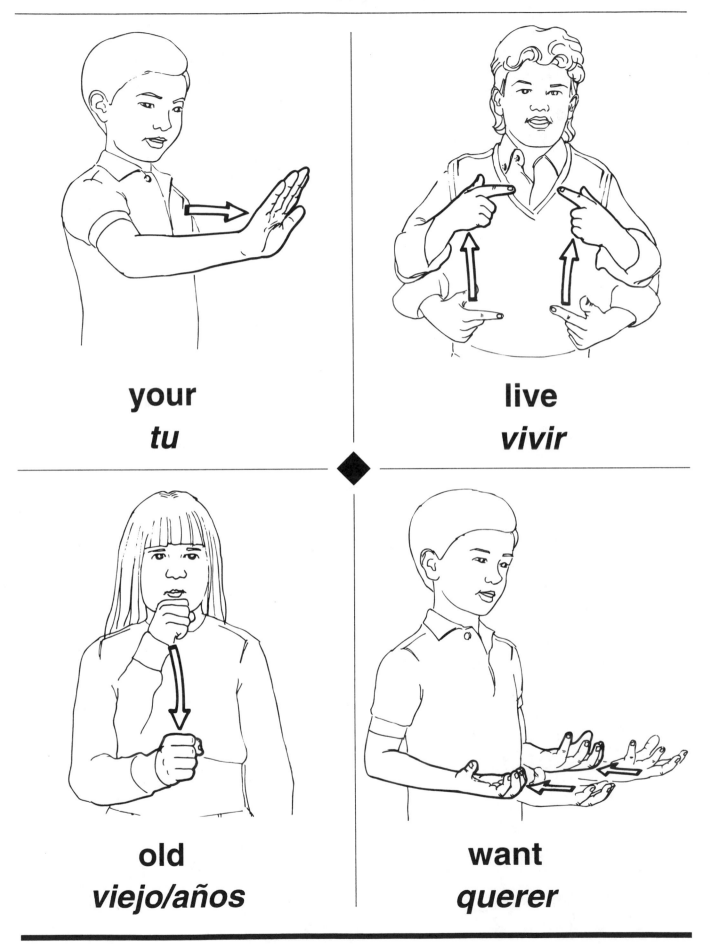

your
tu

live
vivir

old
viejo/años

want
querer

school
escuela

fine
bien

friend
amigo

NAME SIGNS

We

will

invent

some

name

signs!

NOTE TO THE TEACHER

Instead of fingerspelling names of familiar people and places, deaf people use name signs. *There are three ways deaf people determine a name sign for a person or place. The first is by* initialization. *The first letter of a person's name or his or her full initials may be signed in clear view. These signs can be placed on the body above the waist or fingerspelled in the space at the side of the body.*

The signs can be made at the temple, the chin, the chest, the opposite shoulder or the side of the cheek. Name signs for places are often a fingerspelled abbreviation, for example M-D for Maryland, U-S-A for the United States of America.

The second way to determine a name sign is to consider an important characteristic of the person. For example, if a person has large eyes and his or her name starts with the letter R, the name sign could be an R *placed by the corner of the eye. If a person smiles a lot and his or her name begins with* H, *then the name sign could be an* H *placed at the corner of the mouth. For places, the initial of the name for the place can be signed in such a way that would indicate some prominent characteristic of the place. For example, the sign for McDonald's is the signs for* M *and* D *made on the back of the opposite hand in the outline of a golden arch.*

Laura

The last consideration in choosing a name sign is whether a sign already exists for the person's name. For example, a woman named Rose may want to use the sign for the flower rose as her name sign.

Deaf children are typically given name signs by someone in the Deaf community. If you are lucky enough to know people in your local Deaf community invite them to visit your class and help choose name signs for your students. Your students will have a lot of fun learning about and choosing name signs.

Choosing a name sign will be fun for the children. This lesson can be an opportunity to explore the characteristics about themselves that they think are important. You may want to have the students draw pictures of themselves as an extension of this activity. Remember to keep this activity positive. Do not let

children determine a name sign based on a negative characteristic.

The signs for lesson 6 illustrate the actual name signs of the children who modeled for the signs in this book. Sharing that fact with your class will make sign language even more real to the students. After you distribute the handout on name signs, you may want to take Polaroid pictures of the students making their own name signs to include in their sign book. This is also very effective as a bulletin board display.

After your students have decided on their name signs, you could review lesson 5 and incorporate the name signs into the conversation. Keep in mind that when deaf people meet a new person, they fingerspell their names first and then make the name signs that can be used from that point on.

THE LESSON

After discussing how name signs are created, model your name sign. Have the children imitate your name sign until they can do it accurately. Let the children work in small groups to create their own name signs. First, have them state their name and then make the sign. Have practice sessions for children to use their name signs or the name signs of other children. The children can ask, "Who am I?" Then they make their own name sign or the sign for another child. Start using name signs when talking with the children throughout the day. In the beginning, always say the child's name when using the sign.

FOLLOW-UP ACTIVITY

At recess, play "Red Rover" silently signing the children's names instead of saying their names out loud.

NOTES

Angela

Derrick

Billy

Franco

Laura

Sam

Peggy

7

CLASSROOM COOPERATION

Who

wants

to be

a teacher's

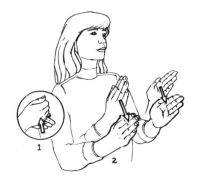

helper?

TARGET VOCABULARY

English/*Spanish*

line up *poner en fila*	finish *terminar*	restroom *retrete*	cooperate *cooperar*
wait *esperar*	stop *parar*	please *por favor*	
sit down *sentarse*	help *ayuda (noun)* *ayudar (verb)*	thank you *gracias*	

NOTE TO THE TEACHER

After you have taught the target vocabulary, you can discuss with the class how signing these words might help the classroom run more smoothly. For example,

signing the request line up *instead of shouting it will help promote a calm and orderly transition from class work to getting ready for lunch. If you are conducting a class lesson and someone needs to go to the bathroom,*

---

the student could silently sign restroom, please, *instead of interrupting, and you can respond with the sign for* yes *or* no *as you continue talking. The class can go on uninterrupted. Ask your class to cooperate (in sign of course) and use signs throughout the day.*

THE LESSON

Tell the children that you are going to use some signs that will be very important to them during the day, and they will be expected to use these signs also. Introduce the target vocabulary. Model each

one several times. Have the children practice them in small groups while you serve as monitor. For the rest of the day, use the signs to communicate with the children. At the end of the day, be sure to review the signs. Distribute the signs for lesson 7.

FOLLOW-UP ACTIVITY

Start a campaign to encourage anyone who is on cafeteria or hall duty to use the cooperation signs. Have the students be the teachers for those who are interested in learning the signs.

NOTES

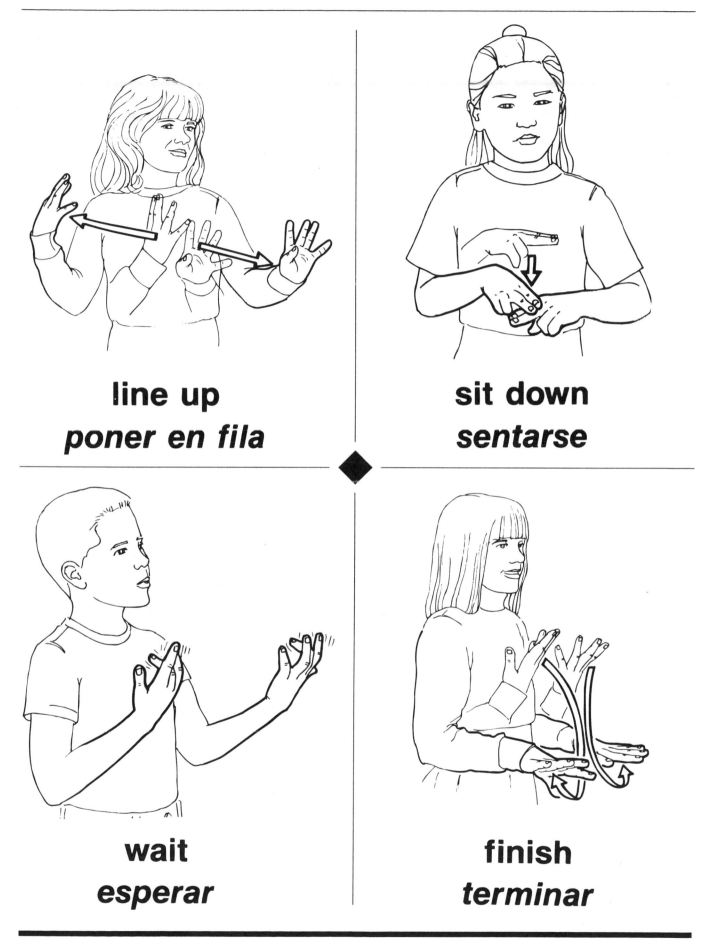

line up
poner en fila

sit down
sentarse

wait
esperar

finish
terminar

stop
parar

restroom
retrete

help
ayuda (noun)
ayudar (very)

please
por favor

thank you
gracias

cooperate
cooperar

8
THE FAMILY

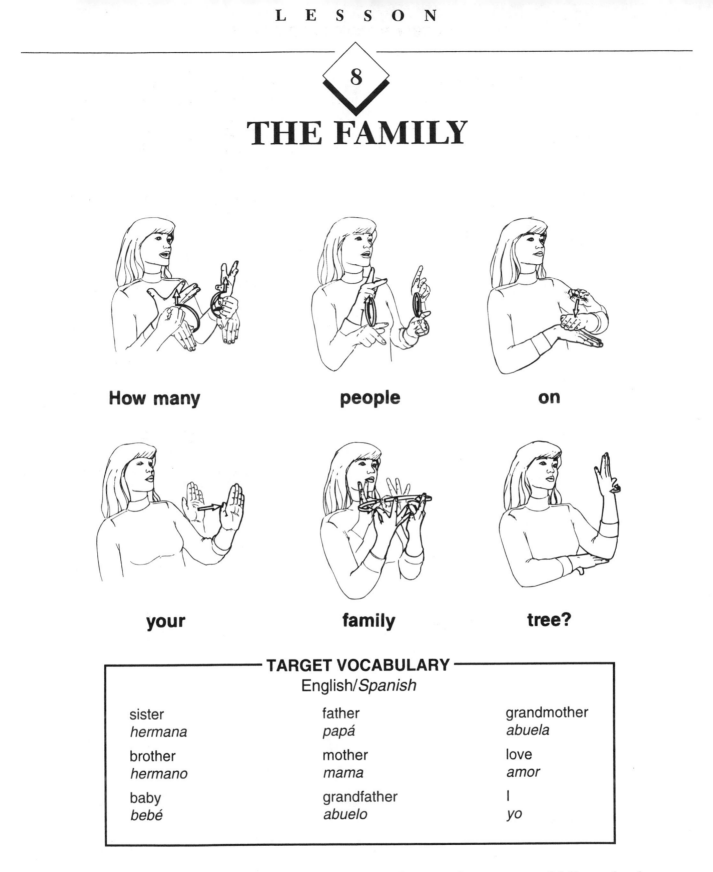

How many	people	on

your	family	tree?

TARGET VOCABULARY
English/*Spanish*

sister	father	grandmother
hermana	*papá*	*abuela*
brother	mother	love
hermano	*mama*	*amor*
baby	grandfather	I
bebé	*abuelo*	*yo*

NOTE TO THE TEACHER

After the lesson is over, distribute the signs for lesson 8. A follow-up activity could be to make a bulletin board with a family tree. Have your students bring in photos or draw pictures of different family members. Have the students cluster them under the appropriate target vocabulary sign. You may cut out the sign illustrations from the handout for this lesson and paste them on the bulletin board as well. The title of the bulletin board could be, Who is on Your Family Tree? Don't forget to include previously learned sign vocabulary in the lesson.

THE LESSON

This lesson on family uses a word-map format. Put the new word *family* in the center on the board. Follow suggestion three (p. 11) and discuss the concept of family. As you do, introduce the signs for the target vocabulary.

CONTEXT ACTIVITY

Pass out cards to the children with sentences containing the target vocabulary. Have a child read the message on the card and sign the bold words. Have the rest of the class guess the message.

Where does your **grandfather** work?
Please ask your **mother** for a cookie.
What does your **sister** want to eat?

Ask the children to make their own sentences using some of the signs they have learned.

FOLLOW-UP ACTIVITY

Have each child create a family tree using whatever materials they choose (paint, chalk, crayons, etc.). Display them on a bulletin board that is captioned with both the printed words and signs from this book. You can enlarge the sign illustrations on a copy machine if you wish.

NOTES

sister
hermana

baby
bebé

brother
hermano

father
papá

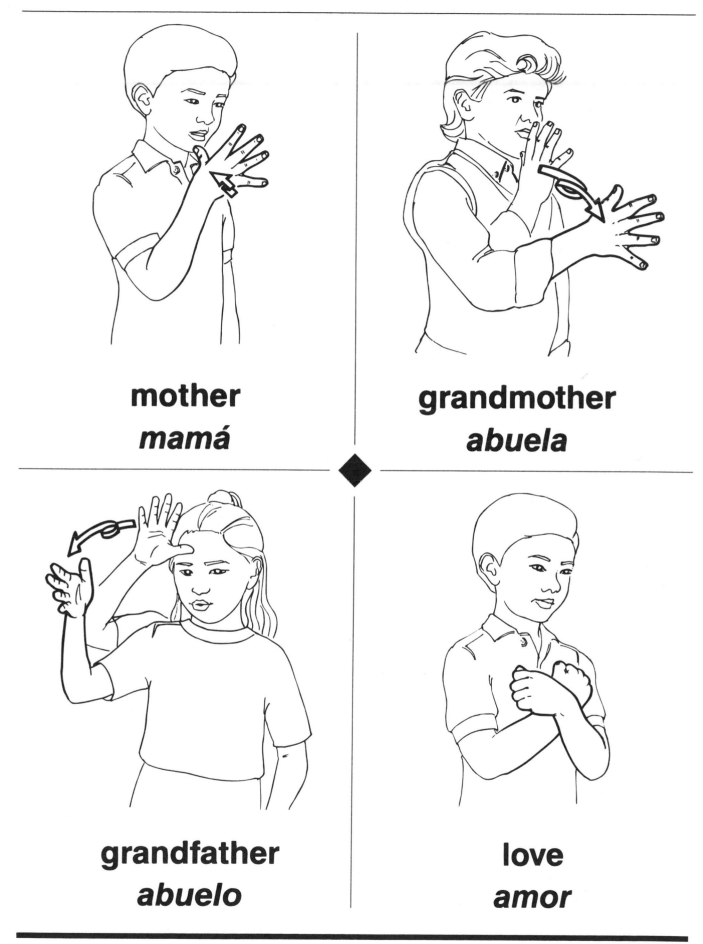

mother
mamá

grandmother
abuela

grandfather
abuelo

love
amor

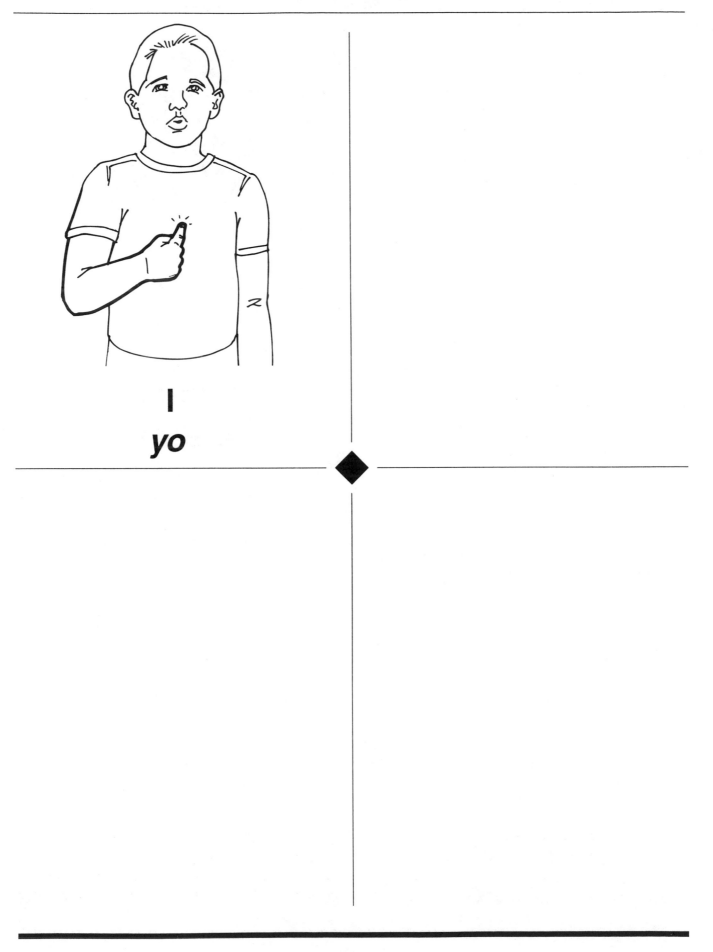

I

yo

OPPOSITES

What

do

you

know

about

opposites?

```
┌──────────── TARGET VOCABULARY ────────────┐
│            English/Spanish                 │
│                                            │
│  same/different    near/far     up/down    │
│  igual/diferente   cerca/lejos  arriba/abajo│
│                                            │
│  tall/short        open/closed  small/big  │
│  alto/bajo         abierto/cerrado (adj.)  pequeño/grande │
│                    abirir/cerrar (verb)    │
│                                            │
│  first/last        hot/cold     on/off     │
│  primero/último    caliente/frío encima/fuera│
└────────────────────────────────────────────┘
```

NOTE TO THE TEACHER

This lesson is conducted using the topic webbing technique (see suggestion four on p. 12). Introduce the concept of opposites however you wish. With younger children you may want to start with pictures. For example, present a picture of something going up (flag on a pole, car on a hill, etc.). Ask the children to show you with their hands the direction the flag is moving. Next, present the picture of down. *Continue this activity using* small/big *and* on/off. *The students will probably gesture very much like the actual signs. After they show you their gesture for each word, show them the sign and comment on how similar the real sign is to the gesture.*

THE LESSON

You are now ready to present the rest of the vocabulary in the web. For younger children, you may want to place "Mr. Opposite Spider" in the center of a web on the board. Tell the children that Mr. Opposite Spider eats only Opposite Bugs. Introduce each target vocabulary word by writing it on a paper bug and then hand the bugs out to the class. Ask who has the *tall* bug, signing the word as you say it. Then ask who has the opposite bug. When the student responds, say and sign the word. As each pair of opposites is introduced, have the students place them together on the web. Review the signs by having a student sign one of the words and then have another student sign the opposite. The rest of the class can respond to the sign by saying the word. Distribute the signs for lesson 9.

CONTEXT ACTIVITY

Pass out cards to the children that contain sentences using the target vocabulary. Have a child read the message on the card and sign the words that appear in bold. The other children should guess what the signed message is.

Is the corn too **hot** or too **cold**?
The restroom is **near** the door.
Your brother is very **tall**.

Ask the children to make their own sentences using some of the signs they have learned. This can be done in a small or large group setting or in pairs.

FOLLOW-UP ACTIVITY

Create a series of sentences that use this sign vocabulary. For example, "A giraffe is a very _____ animal." Write these sentences on sentence strips. As you show them to the class, have the students respond in sign with the missing vocabulary word. You will quickly note who is responding correctly. Repeat the correct response in silence for the students to imitate.

NOTES

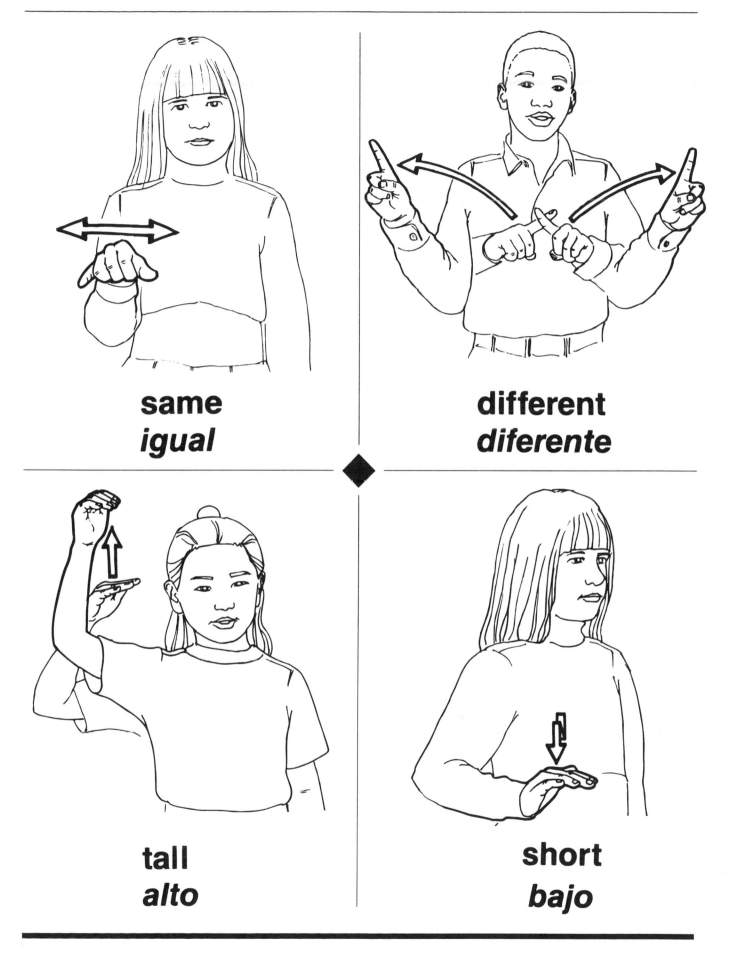

same
igual

different
diferente

tall
alto

short
bajo

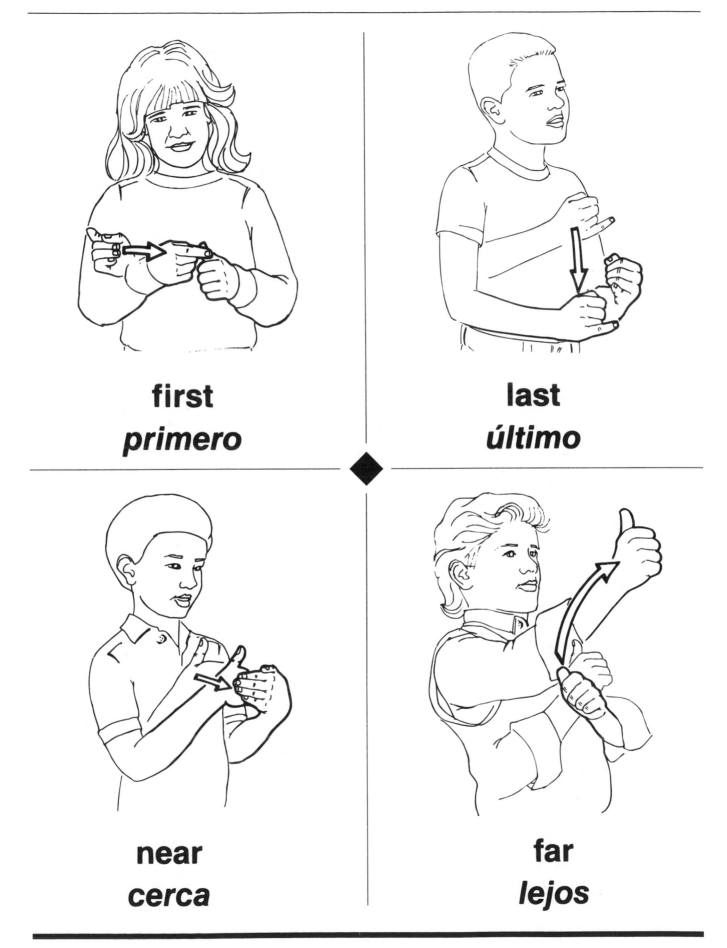

first
primero

last
último

near
cerca

far
lejos

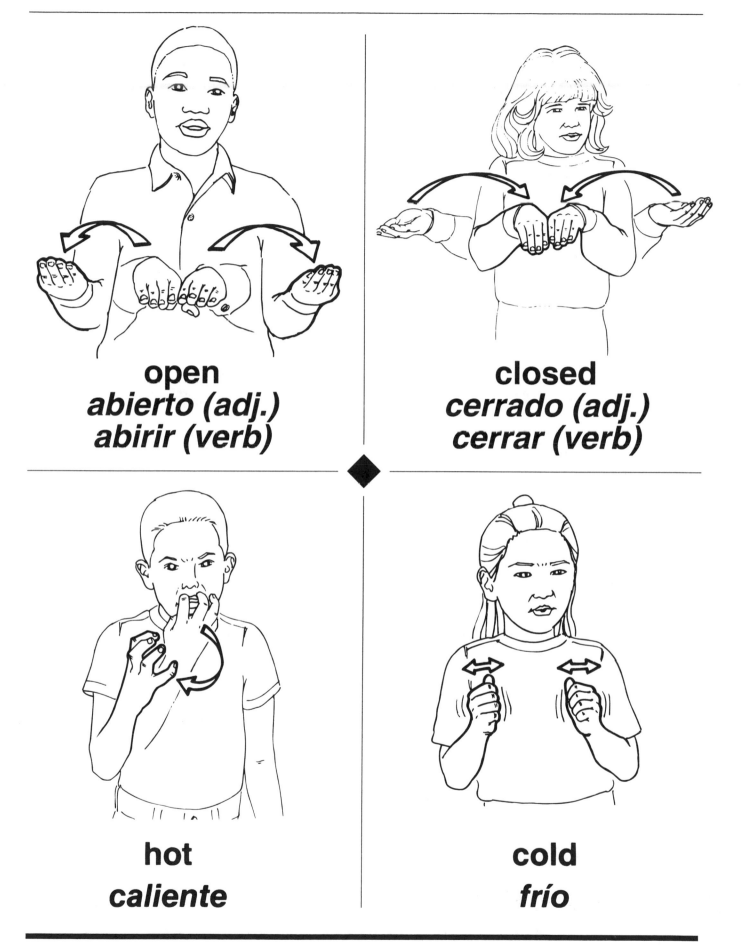

open
abierto (adj.)
abirir (verb)

closed
cerrado (adj.)
cerrar (verb)

hot
caliente

cold
frío

up
arriba

down
abajo

small
pequeño

big
grande

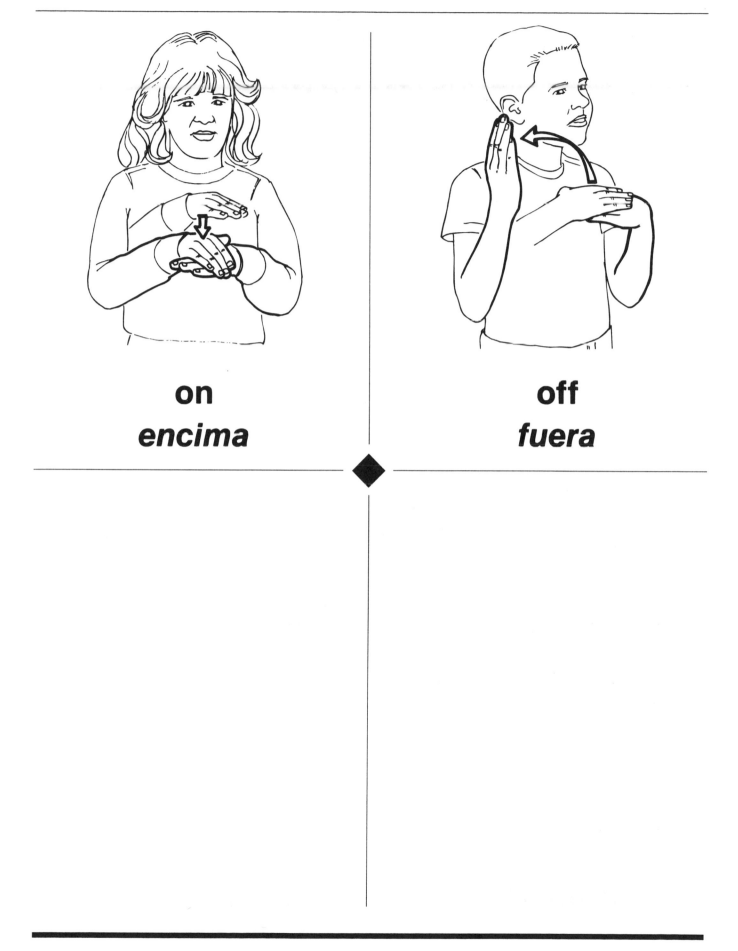

on
encima

off
fuera

10

ACTION WORDS

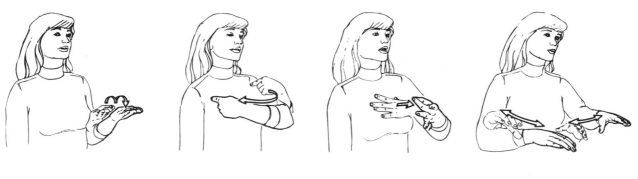

| **Things** | **we** | **like** | **to do.** |

TARGET VOCABULARY

English/*Spanish*

run	fall	read	rest
correr	*caer*	*leer*	*descansar*
walk	sleep	write	
caminar	*dormir*	*escribir*	
jump	eat	play	
brincar	*comer*	*jugar*	

NOTE TO THE TEACHER

Your students will love this lesson because they get to move! Write the target vocabulary words on slips of paper or bring in action pictures illustrating the vocabulary and have the children demonstrate actions for the words. After each action, have them create their own sign for the action.

THE LESSON

Model the correct sign for each of the target words. Compare the students' invented signs with the real sign. Have the children make up sentences using the action words as well as previously learned vocabulary. Distribute the signs for lesson 10.

CONTEXT ACTIVITY

When children read their sentences have them use signs for the words they know. If they don't know the signs for some of the words, they can fingerspell or read the words out loud. Have the other children guess what they are signing.

FOLLOW-UP ACTIVITY

You are halfway through this book! Take the opportunity to review the signs your students have learned so far. Create a vocabulary list of all the signs your class has learned. Have the students write a story using as many vocabulary words as they can (this can be a group-generated story or done by individuals). If this is a group-generated story, divide the sentences among the students. Help students practice signing their sentence(s). If it is an individual activity, you may want to meet in small groups or with each child. Videotape the students signing their stories. Review and discuss them. The students may also want to write and illustrate their stories to take home. Consider inviting the principal or parents to watch the production.

NOTES

run
corcer

jump
brincar

walk
caminar

fall
caer

sleep
dormir

read
leer

eat
comer

write
escribir

play
jugar

rest
descansar

What

sport

do

you

like

best?

TARGET VOCABULARY

English/*Spanish*

football *fútbol americano*	hockey *hockey*	soccer *fútbol*	Olympics *olimpiadas*
basketball *basquetbol*	skateboard *patinar*	tennis *tenis*	
baseball *béisbol*	t-ball *t-ball*	team *equipo*	

NOTE TO THE TEACHER

Have the students sign a sentence using one of the new vocabulary words (for example, Football is fun; I'm on a baseball team; I like tennis best).

THE LESSON

Write the target vocabulary on the board or display pictures. Tell the class you are going to sign each word and that you want them to guess what vocabulary word it is. For younger students, have them silently point or pick up the picture they think you signed. For the older students, have them fingerspell the vocabulary word. After they have had a chance to guess at all the signs, go through them again and model the signs for them. Distribute the signs for lesson 11.

CONTEXT ACTIVITY

Pass out sentence cards containing the target vocabulary. Have a child read the message on the card and sign the bold words. The other children should guess the vocabulary the child is signing. A variation would be to have the child sign the entire sentence. Providing the children with a list of the sign vocabulary they have already learned will help them generate signed sentences.

FOLLOW-UP ACTIVITY

Have each student choose his or her favorite sport. Have them create riddles about their chosen sport. For example, "This sport is rough! Players wear helmets. You can kick, carry, or throw the ball. What sport is it?" Each student should sign his or her riddle, and the other students should sign the answer. Each student could also mime several movements associated with the sport and have the other children sign the name of the sport.

NOTES

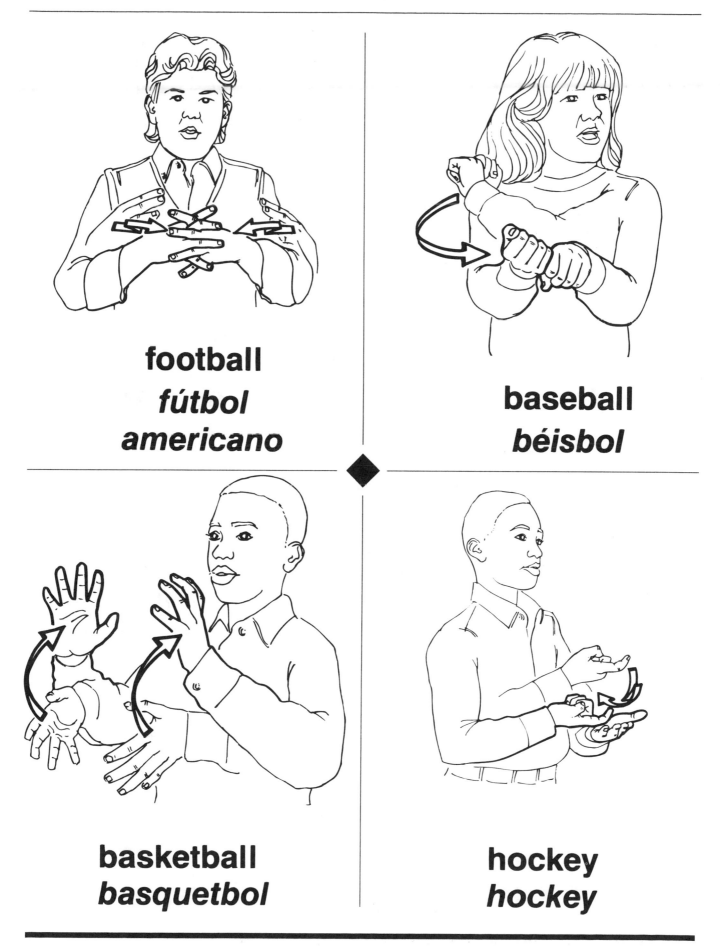

football
fútbol
americano

baseball
béisbol

basketball
basquetbol

hockey
hockey

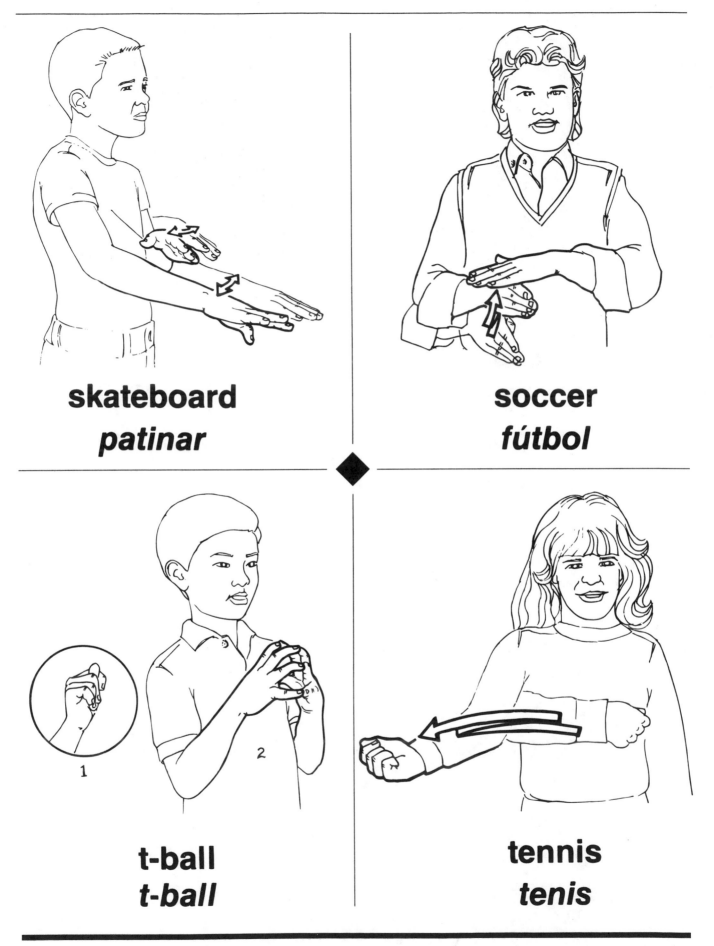

skateboard
patinar

soccer
fútbol

t-ball
t-ball

tennis
tenis

team
equipo

olympics
olimpiadas

12

DAYS OF THE WEEK

  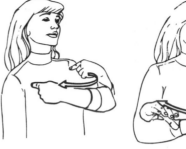 

What   **do**   **we**   **do**

each   **day**   **of the**   **week?**

TARGET VOCABULARY
English/*Spanish*

Sunday	Wednesday	Saturday	special
domingo	*miércoles*	*sábado*	*especial*
Monday	Thursday	day	
lunes	*jueves*	*día*	
Tuesday	Friday	week	
martes	*viernes*	*semana*	

NOTE TO THE TEACHER

The format for this lesson is the circle story (see suggestion six on p. 13). Sequencing is an important concept for developing reading skills. This activity will reinforce sequencing skills while teaching the signs for the days of the week.

THE LESSON

Draw a large circle on the board and divide it into seven parts. If you want to reinforce calendar skills you could draw a large rectangle and divide it into seven parts. Ask the children what the first day of the week is. When they respond, show them the sign for *Sunday* and write it in the first segment of the circle or rectangle. Talk about the activities that the children do on Sunday. Draw a representative picture of the special Sunday activities in the segment. Continue the activity, teaching the signs for each day of the week.

To reinforce calendar skills, teach the ASL sign for *every Monday, every Tuesday*, etc. The sign for Monday is made by moving an *M* from top to bottom of an imaginary calendar in front of you. For the other days, make the same movement using the signs for each day. This is suggestive of the order of the days of the week in a monthly calendar. At the end of lesson, distribute the signs.

CONTEXT ACTIVITY

During the opening exercises each morning have the students use the sign of the day as the calendar is marked off. On Friday when you review the highlights of the week, sign the day as you discuss the activity.

FOLLOW-UP ACTIVITY

Instead of writing the date on the blackboard, try signing the day of the week and date each morning as you conduct opening exercises.

NOTES

Sunday
domingo

Tuesday
martes

Monday
lunes

Wednesday
miércoles

Thursday
jueves

Saturday
sábado

Friday
viernes

day

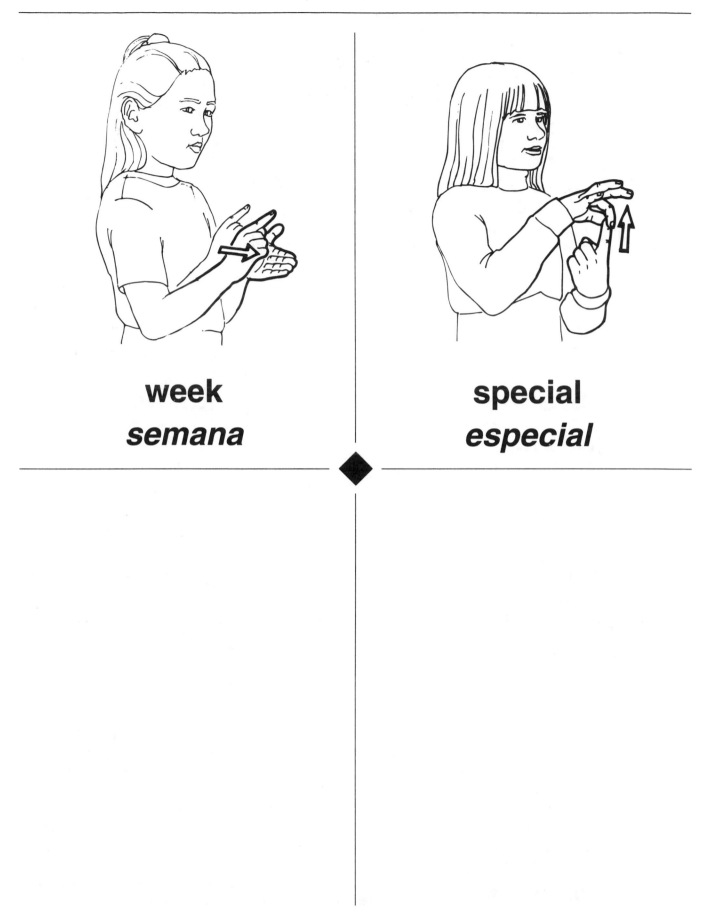

week
semana

special
especial

13

HOLIDAYS

| We | will | celebrate | a happy | holiday |

TARGET VOCABULARY
English/*Spanish*

Halloween *día de brujas*	Hanukkah *Hanukkah*	menorah *menorah*	tree *árbol*
Thanksgiving *día de gracias*	Valentine's Day *día de los enamorados*	jack-o-lantern *linterna de Juan*	fireworks *fuegos artificiales*
Christmas *Navidad*	Independence Day *día de independencia*	turkey *pavo*	sweetheart *enamorado*

NOTE TO THE TEACHER

After all the holiday signs have been learned, sign and say a holiday-related word from the target vocabulary. Ask the students to sign back to you the holiday it relates to. Distribute the signs for lesson 13 and ask the students to write down sentences relating to the holiday theme. Have them sign their sentences to the class.

THE LESSON

This lesson plan uses the format of semantic categories (see suggestion one on p. 10). Sign and say "We will celebrate a happy holiday!" On the chalkboard, write three holidays from the target vocabulary. As you write each one, demonstrate the sign for the holiday. List another holiday and ask the children to demonstrate what they think the sign might be. After a few examples, show them the sign. Ask for more examples of holidays (and be sure to sign your question!).

FOLLOW-UP ACTIVITY

Have students choose a favorite holiday and create a special greeting card. Take pictures of the students signing the holiday. Enclose them inside the card. Mail it to special friends who are aware that your class is learning to sign.

NOTES

Halloween
día de brujas

Christmas
Navidad

Thanksgiving
día de gracias

Hanukkah
Hanukkah

Valentine's Day
día de los
enamorados

menorah
menorah

Independence Day
día de independencia

jack-o-lantern
linterna de Juan

turkey
pavo

fireworks
fuegos artificiales

tree
árbol

sweetheart
enamorado

14

SIGNING SENTENCES

Putting it all together **with** **signs.**

TARGET VOCABULARY

English/*Spanish*

and	can	don't	which
y	*poder*	*no*	*cuál*
but	will	have	
pero		*tener*	
about	I	this	
acerca	*yo*	*esto*	

NOTE TO THE TEACHER

This lesson will add vocabulary that will help your students expand their ability to sign sentences with the signs they already know.

THE LESSON

Create sentences using the target vocabulary for this lesson and previously taught vocabulary. Underline the new target vocabulary word in each sentence. Write these sentences on strips and put them in a hat. Have the students each pick a sentence strip. Tell them to sign all the words in the sentence that they know.

Then, demonstrate the target vocabulary word in each sentence. Ask the class to repeat the sign and then the whole sentence, signing every word. After all of the target vocabulary has been learned, distribute the signs for lesson 14.

FOLLOW-UP ACTIVITY

Create a sign, "**Sign language spoken here**," and post it on your classroom door before the children arrive for school one day. As the children enter the room, greet them in sign only. If they ask a question, answer them in sign only. Encourage them to sign back to you. Soon it will become apparent that your class will be conducted in sign only. Determine how much of the day you can do this. You might decide to only use this activity for the opening exercises. It will depend on the signing skill of your class. This would be a good opportunity to invite a Deaf person to visit and help the students practice their skills. Videotape at least part of the experience. When it is time to resume using spoken language, remove the sign from the door.

NOTES

and
y

about
acerca

but
pero

can
poder

will

don't
no

I
yo

have
tener

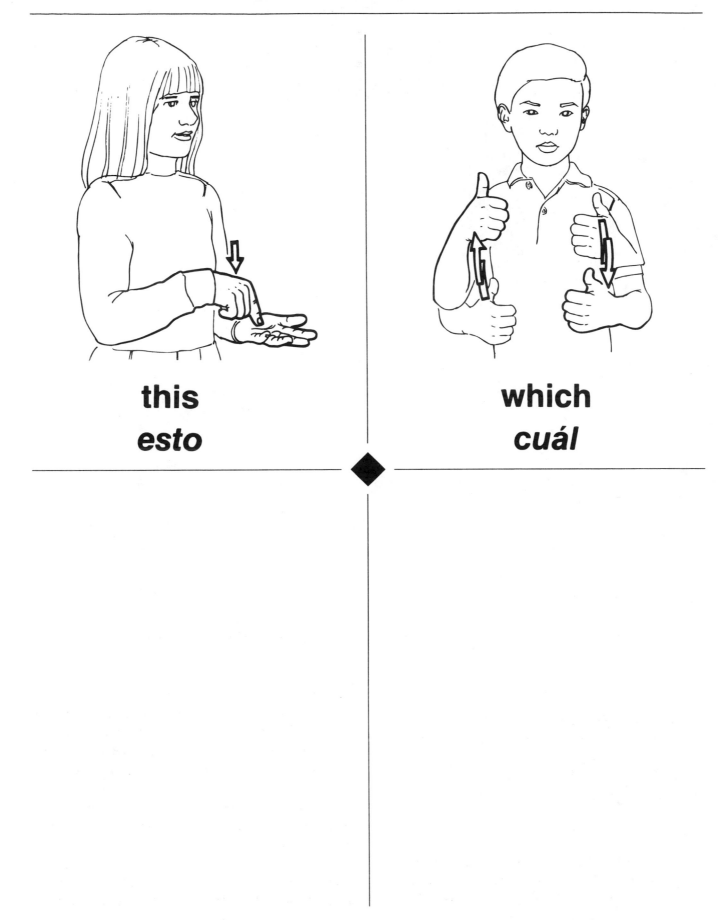

this
esto

which
cuál

ANIMALS

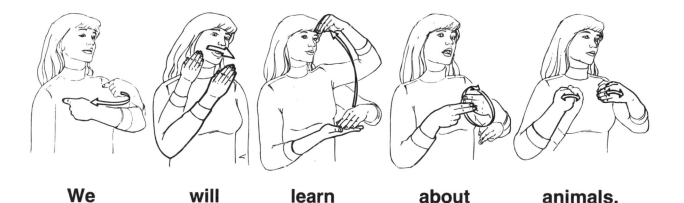

| We | will | learn | about | animals. |

TARGET VOCABULARY
English/*Spanish*

pets *mascotas*	cat *gato*	snake *culebra*	cow *vaca*
dog *perro*	sheep *oveja*	pig *puerco*	bear *oso*
elephant *elefante*	fish *pez*	lion *león*	
farm *finca*	horse *caballo*	rabbit *conejo*	

NOTE TO THE TEACHER

Before you begin this lesson, review the concept of categorizing. Ask the students for an example of a category and its members. The lesson for animals will follow the vocabulary grid format (see suggestion two on p. 10).

THE LESSON

Start with a grid on the board or on a handout. *Sign* your instructions to the children. Sign the vocabulary across the top of the grid first. The students will be using that vocabulary in their responses. Sign each word as you introduce the target vocabulary. Tell the students that as you point to the categories across the top of the grid they should respond with a signed sentence if the animal belongs in that category. Model the first word, *horse*, for them: A horse is a farm animal. After you sign the sentence, check the category. Proceed to the next category (for example, A horse is big.).

After you have introduced all the target vocabulary sing "Old MacDonald's Farm." When you come to the part where you name an animal, point to a student. The student should stand up and *sign* an animal name. Immediately after the student signs the animal, the class should *shout* the word!

Distribute the signs related to this lesson.

FOLLOW-UP ACTIVITY

Help the students develop a skit, "A Trip to the Pet Shop." Some students can portray the animals, some can be customers, and one can be the narrator. Utilize all the mime and sign skills the students have developed to date. Remind the students to fingerspell when they don't know the signs for certain words. Videotape the skit and review it as a group. At this point, you might want to view one of your earlier videotaped activities and compare it with this recent one. Emphasize how the students have improved their signing over time.

NOTES

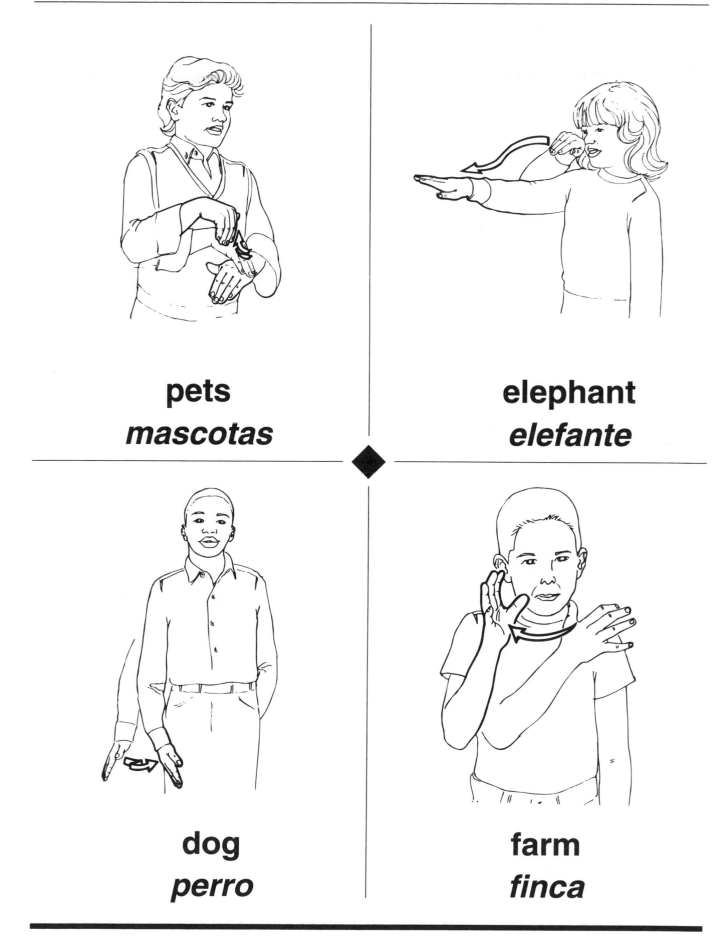

pets
mascotas

elephant
elefante

dog
perro

farm
finca

cat
gato

fish
pez

sheep
oveja

horse
caballo

snake
culebra

lion
león

pig
puerco

rabbit
conejo

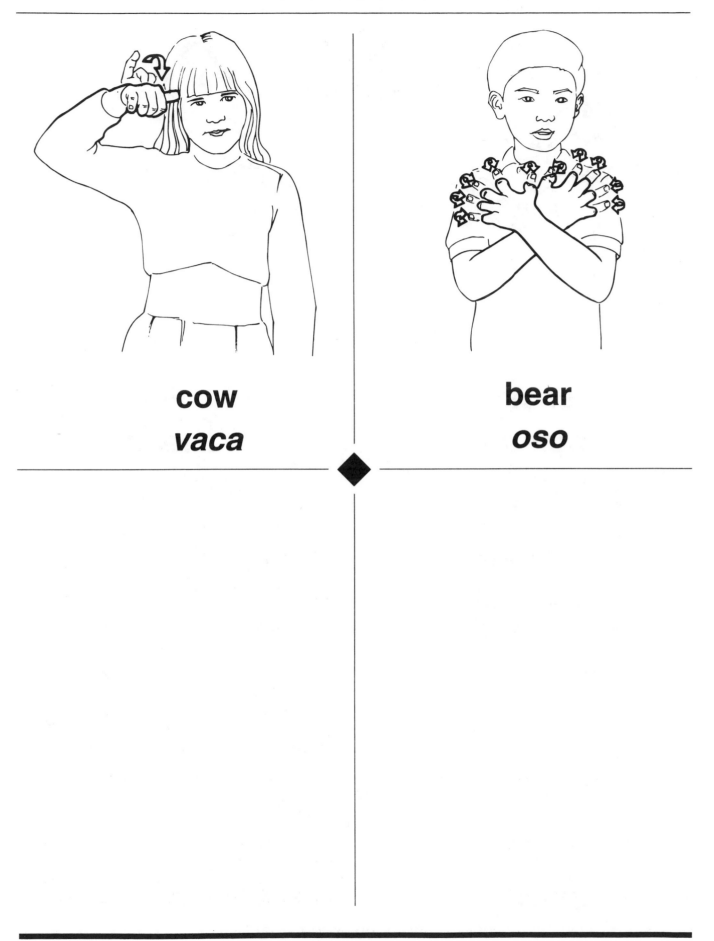

cow
vaca

bear
oso

16

FOOD

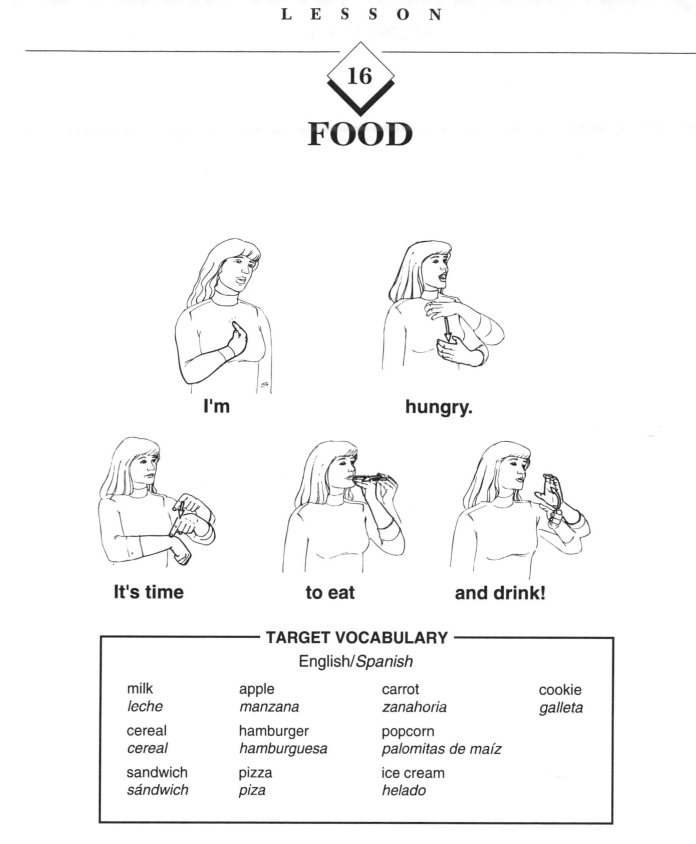

I'm   **hungry.**

It's time   **to eat**   **and drink!**

TARGET VOCABULARY
English/*Spanish*

milk *leche*	apple *manzana*	carrot *zanahoria*	cookie *galleta*
cereal *cereal*	hamburger *hamburguesa*	popcorn *palomitas de maíz*	
sandwich *sándwich*	pizza *piza*	ice cream *helado*	

NOTE TO THE TEACHER

Develop a picture file for the foods included in the target vocabulary. Encourage the students to look through the pictures and sign the foods after you have finished the lesson.

THE LESSON

Sign the sentences, Are you hungry? What do you want to eat? Have pictures of all of the items in the target vocabulary or have the words written on the board. Instruct the children to sign *eat* when they

---

see a picture of the food they would like to eat. Show the food pictures one at a time. When the children sign *eat*, you sign, *You want to eat pizza*. Encourage the children to sign back, *Yes, we want to eat pizza!* Proceed through all the items.

At the end of the lesson distribute the signs for lesson 16.

FOLLOW-UP ACTIVITY

Fingerspell the target vocabulary. After you fingerspell each word, have the students sign the fingerspelled vocabulary. If the students misread a word, simply repeat the fingerspelled word until they respond with the correct sign.

NOTES

milk
leche

sandwich
sándwich

cereal
cereal

apple
manzana

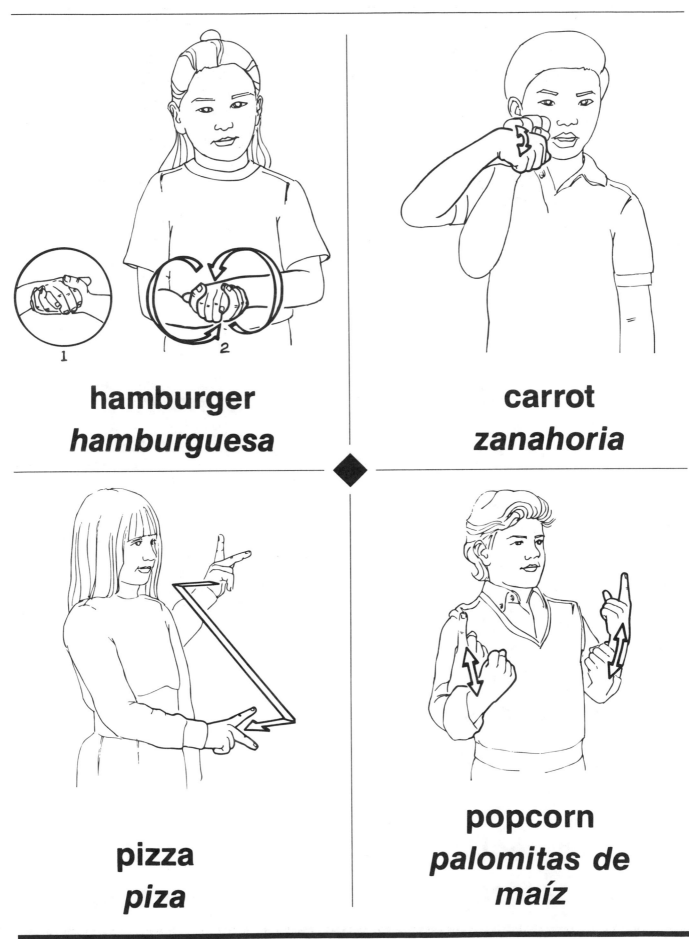

hamburger
hamburguesa

carrot
zanahoria

pizza
piza

popcorn
palomitas de maíz

ice cream
helado

cookie
galleta

17

COLORS

Our

class

will

color

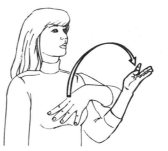

a rainbow.

TARGET VOCABULARY

English/*Spanish*

red	green	brown	crayon
rojo	*verde*	*moreno*	*lápiz de color*
yellow	orange	black	
amarillo	*anaranjado*	*negro*	
blue	purple	white	
azul	*morado*	*blanco*	

NOTE TO THE TEACHER

For this activity, divide your students into color teams. Either assign teams or make it voluntary. You may want to ask the students, "Who wants to be on the red team?" etc. Distribute the corresponding crayon to each team member.

THE LESSON

Tell the students that the class will color a rainbow for the school. Ask the students which crayons their team will use. As they tell you the colors, show them the sign for each color. The students probably will not pick black, brown, and white, but show the students the signs anyway. They can use the signs later.

When everyone has a crayon, proceed with the coloring of the rainbow. Sign, "The red team will now color the rainbow." Continue the activity until all the colors have been used and the rainbow is completed.

Suggest a title for your rainbow. "Sign me a rainbow" would be a possible choice. Have the students cut out the letters for the title and display it with the rainbow. Be ready to hand out the color signs. Assign students to cut out the illustrations for each color in the rainbow.

Ask other students to mount them on the corresponding colors of the rainbow. At the end of the rainbow, have a pot of gold. In the pot of gold place additional copies of the color signs. Underneath the pot of gold write the words, "please take one." Explain to the students that their beautiful rainbow will encourage other children in the school to learn signs.

CONTEXT ACTIVITY

Read the book, *Brown Bear, Brown Bear, What Do You See?* Have the class as a group sign the part, "Brown bear, brown bear, what do you see?" Let each child stand up and sign the response, "I see a _____ looking at me". Have the children read in sign only—no voice.

FOLLOW-UP ACTIVITY

Take this opportunity to practice your Spanish skills! As you say the Spanish word, have the students respond with the corresponding sign, then switch—sign the word and have the students respond with the spoken Spanish word.

NOTES

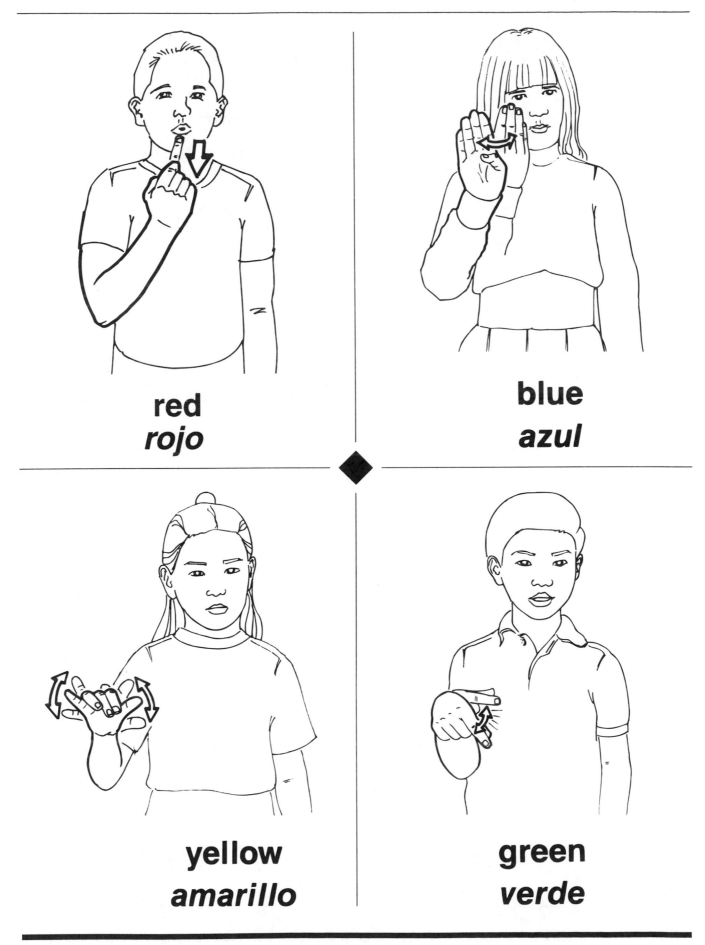

red
rojo

blue
azul

yellow
amarillo

green
verde

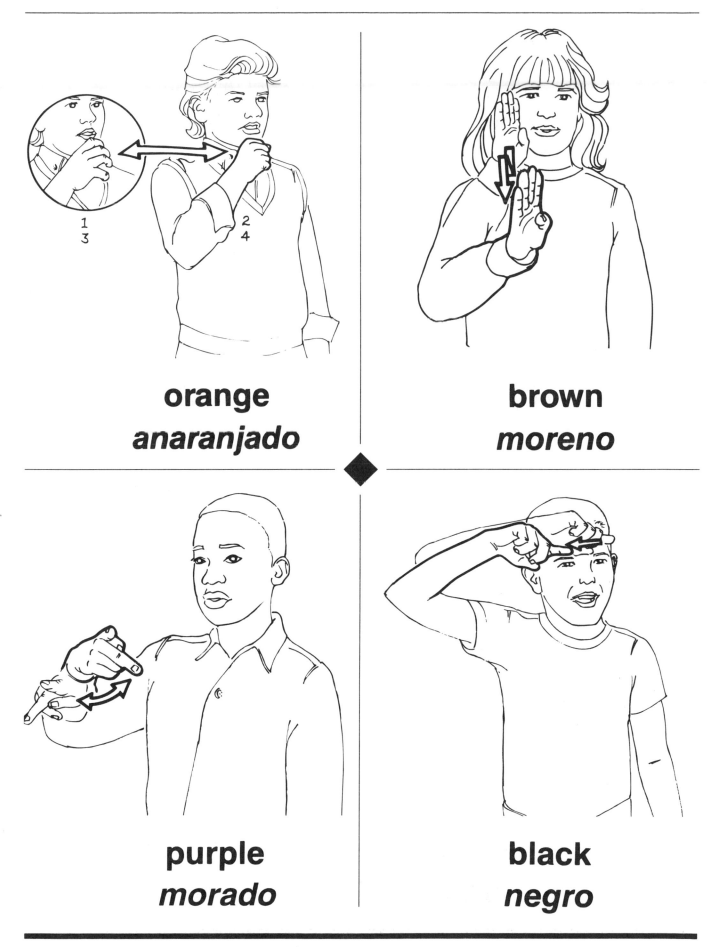

orange
anaranjado

brown
moreno

purple
morado

black
negro

white
blanco

crayon
lápiz de color

TRANSPORTATION

We

will

go

for

a ride

to

Sign

Land!

TARGET VOCABULARY

English/*Spanish*

car *carro*	airplane *avión*	train *tren*	ticket *boleto*
bicycle *bicicleta*	helicopter *helicóptero*	rocket *cohete*	
boat *bote*	motorcycle *motocicleta*	trip *viaje*	

NOTE TO THE TEACHER

Using all your sign vocabulary, tell the students you are going on a trip to Sign Land. Tell them that Sign Land is a beautiful place where everyone talks in sign language! Ask if anyone wants to go on the magical trip with you. Tell them they must have a ticket. Sign the word ticket *as you say it. Collect the imaginary tickets from the students. Encourage them to sign the word* ticket *before they give it to you.*

THE LESSON

Start the trip with everyone driving a car (sign the word). Have the students mime the action of driving a car. On your trip, point out things you see along the way. Encourage students to do the same (in sign, of course). Suddenly your car breaks down (mime something collapsing). Tell the students you must all change vehicles. Now they have to ride bicycles. Use the same procedure, changing vehicles throughout your trip. Finally, you get on a rocket and you reach Sign Land. For the trip home, reverse the order of the vehicles as a review. Ask the students if they enjoyed their trip. As a memento of the visit, give them the signs for lesson 18.

CONTEXT ACTIVITY

Ask the children to make up some sentences that have transportation words in them that they can

sign. Have them take turns and sign the sentences to the class. The other children can respond by writing the sentences on paper as they are signed. At the end of the activity have students self-correct their papers.

FOLLOW-UP ACTIVITY

Young children love picture books about vehicles. Have your class make a picture book using this vocabulary. The book could include drawings or photographs of different vehicles, photographs of the signs, and a short sentence using each vocabulary word. Cover the book with clear plastic. Present it to a kindergarten class in your building during a special ceremony.

NOTES

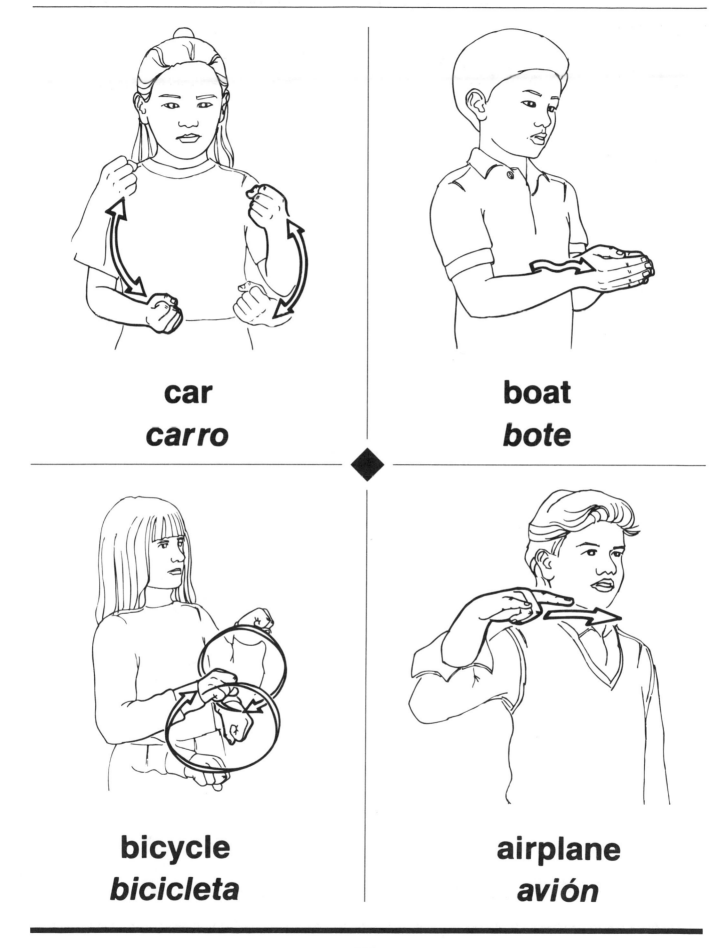

car
carro

boat
bote

bicycle
bicicleta

airplane
avión

helicopter
helicóptero

train
tren

motorcycle
motocicleta

rocket
cohete

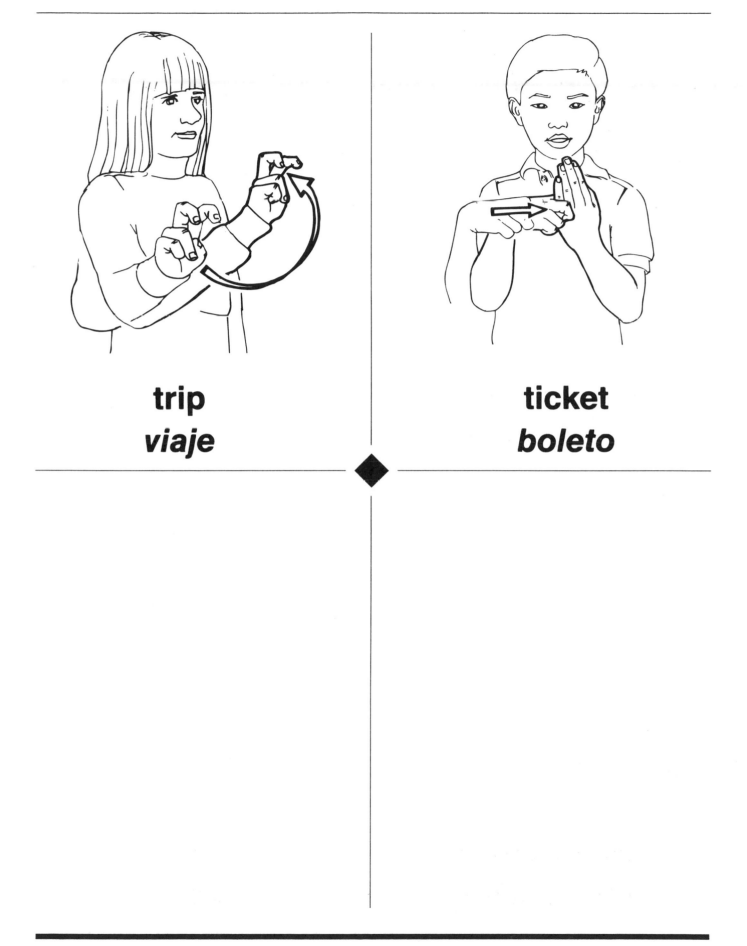

trip
viaje

ticket
boleto

19

MAKE NEW FRIENDS

We   **will**   **sign**   **a song.**

TARGET VOCABULARY

English/*Spanish*

make (meet)	but	is (same)	other
conocer	*pero*	*es*	*otro*
new	keep	silver	gold
nuevo	*guardar*	*plata*	*oro*

NOTE TO THE TEACHER

This is a song that appears in the book, Lift Up Your Hands, *by Donna Gadling Weaks. It would be appropriate in a program for parents or in conjunction with a performance with deaf children.*

THE LESSON

Explain to the children that this is an interpretive version of the song. Even though the English word is *make*, the Spanish translation and the ASL sign is MEET because that is the intended meaning of the lyric. Also, in dramatic, interpretive signing, a signer uses space to make the signs more appealing (see the lyrics, "one is silver and the other's gold").

Distribute the signs for lesson 19 and have the children practice reading the sign lyrics as they would any song lyrics. If you wish, accompany the practice with a piano or other instrument.

FOLLOW-UP ACTIVITY

Take the opportunity to perform this song for an audience. It would be nice for a PTA meeting, a school assembly, or a special "present" performed for each class at the end of the school year. Videotape it and give a copy to the music teacher for her reference library.

NOTES

MAKE NEW FRIENDS

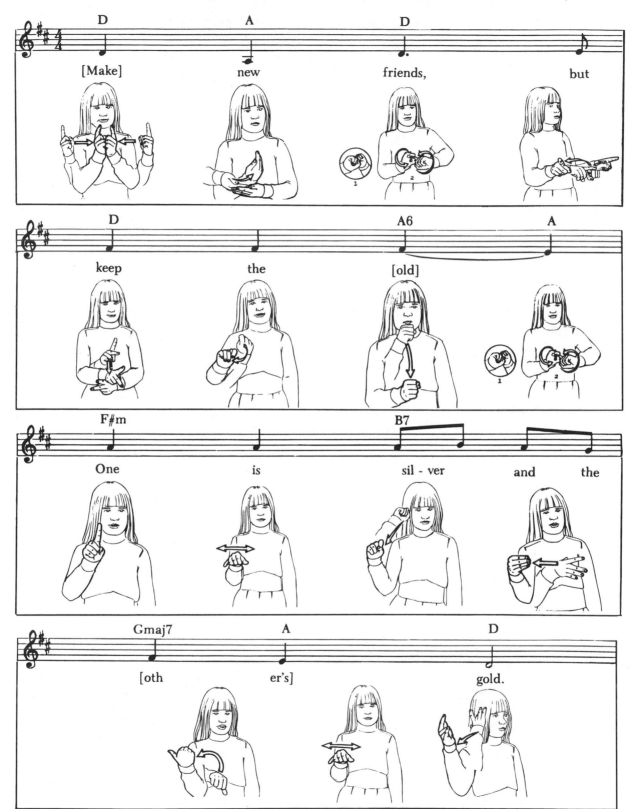

Source: *Lift Up Your Hands Songbook,* © 1976, published by the National Grange, 1616 H Street NW, Washington, DC 20006. Used by permission.

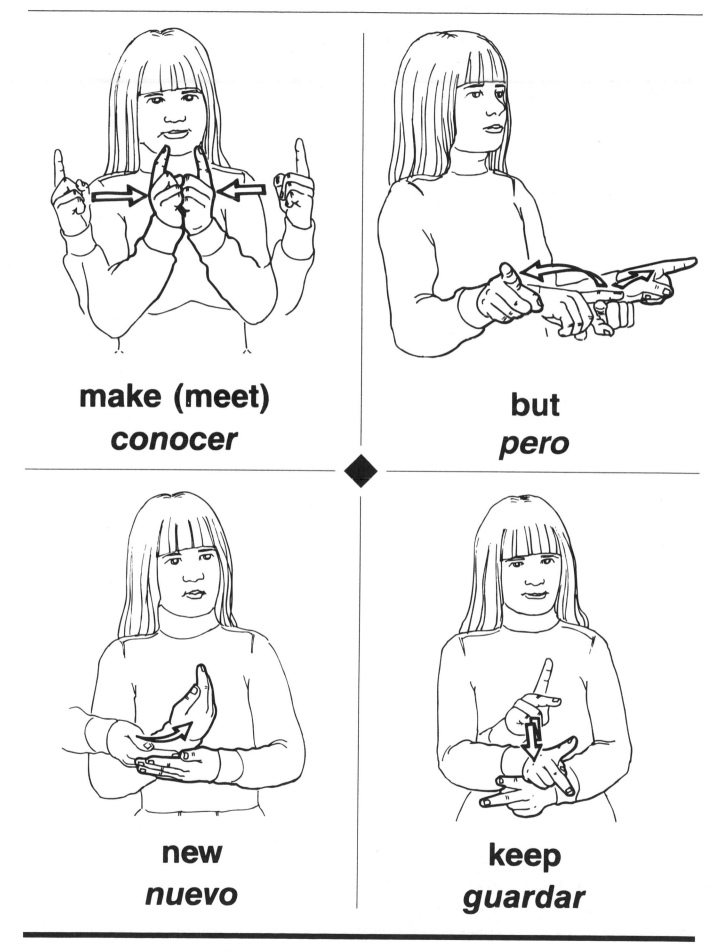

make (meet)
conocer

but
pero

new
nuevo

keep
guardar

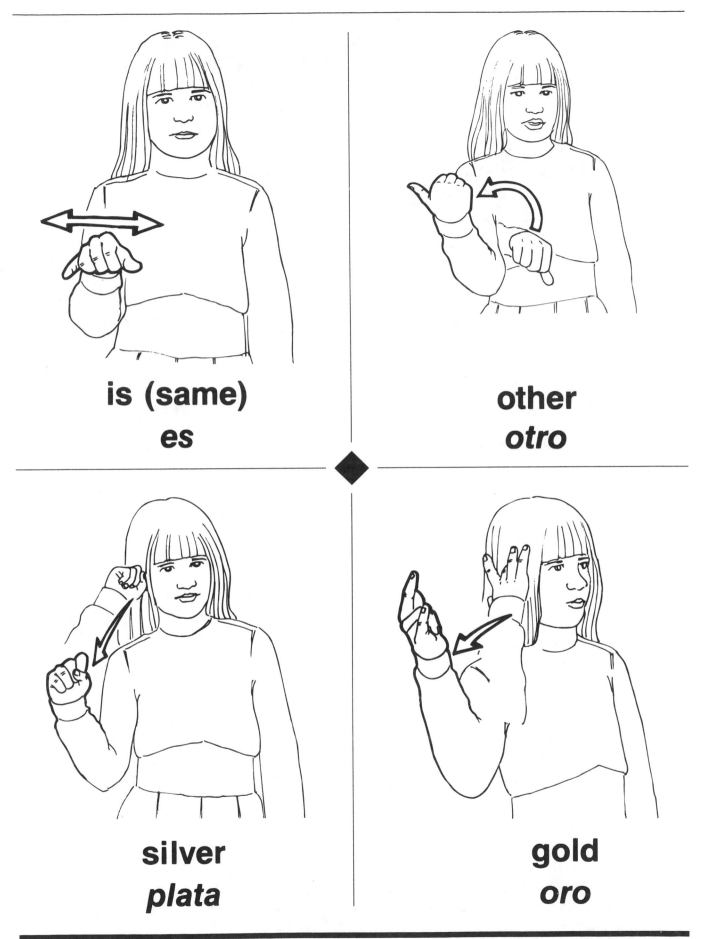

is (same)
es

other
otro

silver
plata

gold
oro

20

COMMUNICATION

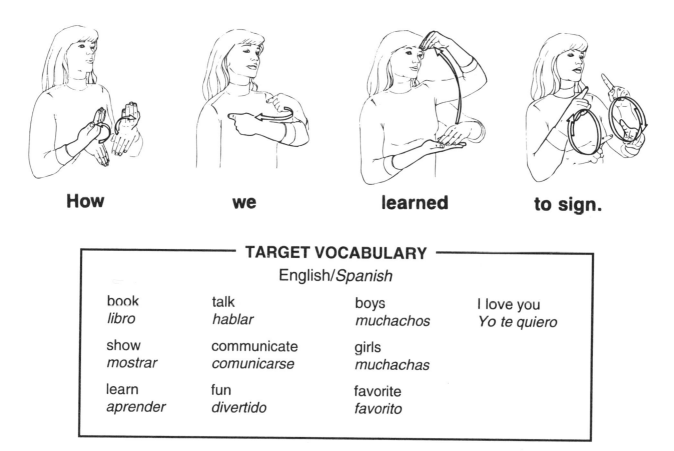

How   **we**   **learned**   **to sign.**

TARGET VOCABULARY
English/*Spanish*

book	talk	boys	I love you
libro	*hablar*	*muchachos*	*Yo te quiero*
show	communicate	girls	
mostrar	*comunicarse*	*muchachas*	
learn	fun	favorite	
aprender	*divertido*	*favorito*	

NOTE TO THE TEACHER

This lesson follows the personal outlining format described in suggestion five on p. 12. Before you begin the personal outlining strategy, have your class write a language experience story about learning sign language. Be sure to include the target vocabulary for this lesson as well as previously taught sign vocabulary. When you have written the story, ask the students to sign the story. When they come to one of the target vocabulary words show them the sign.

THE LESSON

Help your students outline the story in as much detail as they can understand. When you have completed the activity, distribute the signs for lesson 20. Have the students copy (or you may want to distribute photocopies) the story to add to their sign book. Encourage the students to sign the story to their families. You may also want to share this story with a class for the deaf in your school or with whom you correspond. You can also have a student read the story at the next school program and then have your class sign a song.

FOLLOW-UP ACTIVITY

Often, Deaf and hearing people get together for a "silent supper." This is a favorite activity for adult sign classes. Plan to invite Deaf children or adults you may know for lunch at school. If you do not know any Deaf people, just eat lunch together as a class and sign only. No talking is allowed. Afterwards, discuss how the class felt about the experience.

NOTES

book
libro

learn
aprender

show
mostrar

talk
hablar

communicate
comunicarse

boys
muchachos

fun
divertido

girls
muchachas

favorite
favorito

I love you
Yo te quiero

CREATIVE USES OF SIGNING

Once students have developed some signing skills, they will be anxious to use them to communicate with others. This chapter will discuss some of the possible creative activities, projects, and programs that teachers can implement to help children share what they have learned about signing.

COMMUNICATING WITH DEAF CHILDREN

Perhaps the most rewarding activity for new signers is to use their signing skills to become friends with deaf children. Deaf children are everywhere. They can be found in schools for the deaf and in public schools. They will be found in churches, playgrounds, and various youth organizations. If you cannot locate any deaf children, ask the special education teachers and speech and hearing therapists in your school for help. Once you've located some deaf children, try the following activities with your students.

Video Letters

Have your class send video letters (letters signed on videotape) to a class of deaf children that you have located. Your class could develop a story using newly learned signs, create a poem, or just send a chatty letter. The video letter can be sent along with a written letter of the same message. Have the children introduce themselves by fingerspelling and then signing their names. Then let them ask questions of the deaf children and request a video letter in reply.

Field Trips

By arranging a visit to a class for deaf children or the state school for the deaf, hearing children can use their signing in a "real life" communication setting. Some preparation will aid in making this a positive experience for all of the children involved.

1. Prepare your students to introduce themselves.

2. Your students might have difficulty interpreting the signs of the deaf children, so let them know that it's all right to ask for something to be repeated or for help.

3. Some of the deaf children will want to communicate without signs with your students and their speech might be difficult to understand, at first. Encourage your students to be patient. They will quickly pick up on the oral language of the deaf children. Inform your students that deaf children cannot monitor their own speech in the same way that hearing children do, so it might sound a little unusual at first.

4. Encourage your students to communicate in a way they are comfortable with. Some students may prefer to talk when they sign; others may wish to try signing without using their voice.

Visits to your Classroom

By asking deaf children to visit your classroom, the field trip idea is reversed. Now the deaf children get an opportunity to visit a hearing classroom in which they will find hearing children who know some signs. It might be best to organize the visit around an activity such as making cookies or painting a mural. If you know in advance that the deaf children are studying the same topics in science or social studies that your hearing students are studying, then the content for that visit can be very meaningful and key signs about that content can be learned before the deaf guests arrive. The same preparation steps as mentioned earlier for field trips can be used.

SPECIAL SCHOOL PROGRAMS

School assemblies or special programs are excellent places for children to share their newly learned signing skills. It is our experience that other children become very interested in the signs and are eager to learn them also. These programs can include the following activities.

Pledge of Allegiance

Children who have learned the signs for the Pledge of Allegiance can lead the other children in an opening ceremony for a school assembly. At first, the children might just use the key words until all of the children have learned them. Then other words can be introduced. Children who sign the Pledge of Allegiance develop a new and rich understanding of it.

Songs

Many songs have sheet music with the signs on the sheet music, so it is rather easy for children to learn to sign the songs as they sing them. We have seen kindergarten children sing *America the Beautiful* while signing the words. It creates a very moving and meaningful presentation. Other songs are equally easy to learn to sign. One school had sixth graders stand on the stage behind first graders and both groups signed several songs together. This type of program reinforces the idea that signing is for everyone.

Nursery Rhymes

When some of your students have learned a nursery rhyme, let them sign it and have the other students guess what the nursery rhyme is. Then, while the signers sign it, all children can repeat the nursery rhyme. Then take the children to visit a kindergarten or preschool class to share some signs with them by signing some traditional nursery rhymes.

Plays

While some students act out a play and sign their parts, a narrator can read the play. In this way the audience can see the play and the signs while listening to the narrator. Such plays can be very short and repeated several times so that the audience can learn the signs. A brief introduction of the key signs can be conducted before the play begins and those same signs can be reviewed at the end of the play.

SIGN CLUBS

Many schools have started sign clubs that meet during school hours or after school. It has been our experience that children become very enthusiastic about joining a sign club. Members of the club can take part in the school programs already mentioned and can serve as motivators for others to learn sign language. Sign club members can learn words in categories like those presented in this book, in songs, in stories, and in plays. The members can develop posters that promote an understanding of signing, and they can serve as leaders for field trips or visits to other schools.

PARENT MEETINGS

Teachers are often looking for a program that communicates to parents what is going on in school. A demonstration of signing learned in school suits that purpose very well. Children can sign some songs, the alphabet, days of the week, or other sign activities that they have worked on in school. Parents are very receptive to such programs, which afford the teacher an opportunity to show what has been learned and a chance to discuss the reasons for it.

CELEBRATE DEAF AWARENESS WEEK

Deaf Awareness Week is celebrated during the last week of
September each year. Use this designated week to help others
become aware of deafness through your various sign activities. This
might be a good week to have deaf visitors come to your school to
participate in mainstreamed activities. Your students can make
posters about deafness and signing that can be featured in the school.
Perhaps all teachers and children could learn several signs during the
week and use them. Signs such as *line up, thank you, I love you,* and
hello could be used throughout the school all week long.

ANNOTATED BIBLIOGRAPHY

MATERIALS FOR CHILDREN

Sign Language Materials

ABC Come Sign with Me. Greensboro, N.C.: Sugar Sign Press. This ABC frieze illustrates the manual alphabet. Nice for a classroom display on sign language.

Bahan, Ben, and Joe Dannis. *My ABC Signs of Animal Friends*. San Diego: DawnSign Press, 1994. A sign language primer for young children. Includes the manual alphabet and signs for twenty-six animals.

Bahan, Ben, and Joe Dannis. *Signs for Me: Basic Vocabulary for Children, Parents and Teachers*. San Diego: DawnSign Press, 1994. An outstanding ASL/English vocabulary reference. Includes 300 words. Index is translated in six languages: Spanish, Vietnamese, Hmong, Tagalog, Lao, and Cambodian.

Baker, Pamela J. *My First Book of Sign*. Washington, D.C.: Gallaudet University Press, 1986. An alphabet book illustrating 150 signs frequently used by children. The words are grouped alphabetically by category (nouns, verbs, modifiers).

Bornstein, Harry, and Karen Saulnier. *Goldilocks and the Three Bears, Little Red Riding Hood, The Night Before Christmas*, and *Nursery Rhymes from Mother Goose*. Washington, D.C.: Gallaudet University Press. Favorite children's stories are told with word-for-word translation into Signed English and accompanied by full-color illustrations.

Bornstein, Harry, and Karen Saulnier. *The Signed English Starter*. Washington, D.C.: Gallaudet University Press, 1986. A beginning reference for Signed English instruction. The signs are grouped by categories with practice sentences at the end of each section.

Bornstein, Harry, Karen L. Saulnier, and Lillian Hamilton. *The Comprehensive Signed English Dictionary*. Washington, D.C.: Gallaudet University Press, 1983. A dictionary with more than 3,100 signs, including the American Manual Alphabet, manual numbers, and sign markers used in Signed English. There is a section on how to choose name signs for friends and family.

Bornstein, Harry, Karen Saulnier, et al. *Signed English Children's Books*. Washington, D.C.: Gallaudet University Press. 23 books. Beginning books (9 books) are intended to help children learn about daily experiences (dressing, playing, eating, etc.) and about topics of interest to them (animals, toys, colors, etc.). Growing up books (6 books) include stories that describe high-interest topics (going to the farm, the holidays, etc.). Stories and Poems (7 books) are written on a more complex linguistic and conceptual level. Titles include *Jack and the Beanstalk, The Three Little Pigs,* and *The Ugly Duckling.*

Chaplin, Susan. *I Can Sign My ABCs.* Washington, D.C.: Gallaudet University Press, 1986. An alphabet picture book that has twenty-six signs, one for each letter of the alphabet. The illustrations are charming.

Johnson, Sue. *At Grandma's House.* Los Alamitos, Calif.: Modern Signs Press, 1985. A short story about Grandma, illustrated with familiar signs.

Manual Alphabet Poster. Washington, D.C.: Gallaudet University Press. This poster would be a colorful addition to any classroom display on sign language.

Sesame Street Sign Language ABC with Linda Bove. New York: Random House, 1985. Deaf actress Linda Bove and the Sesame Street Muppets sign the alphabet and select vocabulary.

Shroyer, Susan, and Joan Kimmel. *ABC Sign With Me.* Greensboro, N.C.: Sugar Sign Press, 1987. This colorful alphabet book presents the twenty-six letters of the manual alphabet. Each letter is illustrated by a color picture of an object that begins with the corresponding letter. The book is laminated to withstand lots of use.

Shroyer, Susan, and Joan Kimmel. *1 2 3 Sign With Me.* Greensboro, N.C.: Sugar Sign Press, 1987. This book teaches the numerals 1–10 and their manual counterparts. The four basic shapes taught in preschool (circle, square, triangle, and rectangle) are included. A nice feature is that the signs for the objects are presented with the numbers included in the back of the book. The book is laminated for durability.

Shroyer, Susan, and Joan Kimmel. *Secret Signing.* Greensboro, N.C.: Sugar Sign Press, 1988. These two books (pre-K and grades 1–3) are activity books to reinforce sign skills. Activities include dot-to-dot pictures, mazes, and matching games. Teachers can reproduce the activity sheets for the classroom. These are great supplements to sign language lesson plans.

Shroyer, Susan, and Joan Kimmel. *Sign With Me Colors.* Greensboro, N.C.: Sugar Sign Press, 1987. This book teaches the eleven basic color signs as well as twelve additional signs for the accompanying vocabulary.

Shroyer, Susan, and Joan Kimmel. *Sign With Me Weather.* Greensboro, N.C.: Sugar Sign Press, 1987. Print, picture, and signs are presented for ten weather concepts. At the end of the book are additional signs for sign markers for changing the form of the basic sign.

Slier, Debby. *Word Signs: A First Book of Sign Language* and *Animal Signs: A First Book of Sign Language.* Washington, D.C.: Gallaudet University Press, 1995. Board books featuring photos of babies and animals, and illustrations of signs for basic vocabulary appealing to very young children.

Wojcer, M. David; developed by Gerilee Gustason, and Esther Zowolkow. *Music in Motion.* Los Alamitos, Calif.: Modern Signs Press, 1983. A songbook for children that features twenty-two familiar songs illustrated in signs. The signs are from the Signing Exact English vocabulary.

Coloring Books

Bornstein, Harry, and Karen Saulnier. Washington, D.C.: Gallaudet University Press. *Don't Be a Grumpy Bear*.

Miller, Ralph, Betty Miller, and Frank Allen Paul. *Sign Language Fun, Sign Language House, Sign Language Clowns, Sign Language Animals*, and *Sign Language Feelings*. Berkeley, Calif.: DawnSign Press. Books include the fingerspelled word as well as the sign illustration.

Storybooks

Charlip, Remy, Mary Beth Miller, and George Ancona. *Handtalk Birthday*. New York: Macmillan/Four Winds Press, 1987. This is a fun-filled story about Mary Beth's surprise birthday party. The basic signs for vocabulary related to the birthday party theme are presented in beautiful full-color photographs. A must for your sign language library.

Levi, Dorothy Hoffman. *A Very Special Friend*. Washington, D.C.: Gallaudet University Press, 1989. A delightful story of the friendship that develops between two six-year-olds—one hearing and one deaf.

Levi, Dorothy Hoffman. *A Very Special Sister*. Washington, D.C.: Gallaudet University Press, 1992. A sequel that explores a deaf child's feelings about having a new, and possibly hearing, sibling.

Levine, Edna. *Lisa and Her Soundless World*. New York: Human Sciences Press, 1974. A wonderful introduction to deafness for children. Using a hearing aid, reading lips, and signing are incorporated into the story about Lisa.

Litchfield, Ada. *Words in Our Hands*. Chicago: Albert Whitman, 1980. The story of a little boy whose parents are deaf. The ways that deaf people adapt to everyday situations are told through the story.

MacKinnon, Christy. *Silent Observer*. Washington, D.C.: Gallaudet University Press, 1993. A lovely, true story of a deaf girl's life at the turn of the twentieth century. Subtle view of growing up in a visual world.

Peterson, Jeanne. *I Have A Sister, My Sister Is Deaf*. New York: Harper and Row, 1977. A touching story about a young deaf girl and her older sister. Illustrates how deaf children are more like hearing children than different.

Additional Instructional Materials

Children's Sign Language Playing Cards. Children can play games such as "Old Maid," "Go Fish," and "Concentration" while they learn sign language. Great for a free-time activity for the classroom or learning center. Available from the Deafness Gallery at Gallaudet University.

The Fantastic Series. Washington, D.C.: Gallaudet University, 8 videotapes. A videotape series that encourages use of imagination. Includes signed stories and mime. Captioned and voice over. Available from Gallaudet University Press.

Four for You: Fables and Fairy Tales. Performed by Lou Fant, Freda Norman, Mary Beth Miller, and Patrick Graybill. Burtonsville, Md.: Sign Media, Inc., 5 vols. Each videotape includes several fables and two fairy tales.

High Five: Fables and Fairy Tales. Performed by Lou Fant, Freda Norman, Mary Beth Miller, Patrick Graybill, and Bill Ennis. Burtonsville, Md.: Sign Media, Inc., 5 vols. Each videotape includes several fables and two fairy tales.

I Love You Self-inking Stamp. Available from the Deafness Gallery at Gallaudet University.

Keep Quiet. This is a timed game that challenges players to create as many words as possible with the manual alphabet in a crossword format; for ages seven to adult. Available from the Deafness Gallery at Gallaudet University.

Manual Alphabet Rubber Stamp Set. A set of manual alphabet hand stamps can be a great addition to the classroom for making learning materials. Available from the Deafness Gallery at Gallaudet University.

Once Upon a Time. . . . Children's Classics Retold in American Sign Language. Signed by Ben Bahan and Nathie Marbury. San Diego: DawnSign Press, 6 sets (video and storybook). Videotapes of stories told in ASL accompanied by English in the storybook. Includes sign glossary.

Sign-Me-A-Story. Signed by Linda Bove. Sony Video. The thirty-minute videotape includes two stories told in ASL—"Little Red Riding Hood" and "Goldilocks and the Three Bears."

Visual Tales. Signed by Billy Seago. Sign-A-Vision. These videotapes are an entertaining way to introduce children to signing—either ASL or Signed English. Each twelve-minute tape includes a teacher/student resource packet. Titles include *The Greedy Cat, The Magic Pot, The House That Jack Built, Village Stew*, and *The Father, the Son, and the Donkey*.

Materials on Deafness for the Teacher

The Ear and Hearing. Washington D.C.: National Information Center on Deafness, Gallaudet University. This pamphlet explains about the anatomy of the ear, how humans hear, and how to protect hearing.

Growing Up Without Hearing. Washington, D.C.: National Information Center on Deafness, Gallaudet University. This twelve-page booklet describes the lives of four deaf and hearing-impaired children. Communication and education differences are illustrated.

Hafer, Jan, and Robert Wilson. *Signing for Reading Success*. Washington, D.C.: Gallaudet University Press, 1986. A guide for incorporating signs and fingerspelling into reading and language arts lessons.

How Deaf People Communicate. Washington, D.C.: National Information Center on Deafness, Gallaudet University. This publication introduces the ways that deaf people communicate, including speechreading, signing, and Cued Speech. Illustrations of signs are included.

MATERIALS FOR ADULTS

Sign Language Texts

Costello, Elaine. *Religious Signing: A Comprehensive Guide for All Faiths*. Rev. ed. New York: Bantam Books, 1986. More than 500 signs necessary for clear communication in religious settings are included in this book. It also has a section on favorite verses, prayers, and blessings.

Costello, Elaine. *Say It by Signing: A Video Guide to the Basics of Sign Language*. New York: Crown Publishers, 1985. 60 minutes. This videotape presents sign language lessons in four sections: family and friends, going out, food and drink, and shopping. English captions are included. Excellent for studying at student's own pace and seeing a variety of people signing.

Costello, Elaine. *Signing: How to Speak With Your Hands*. 2d ed. New York: Bantam Books, 1995. An excellent text for learning American Sign Language. Explanations of linguistic principles and a short history of sign language and deaf people are included.

Fant, Lou. *The American Sign Language Phrase Book*. rev. ed. Chicago: Contemporary Books, 1994. Everyday expressions of ASL are presented in this easy to use text. Designed to allow students to use ASL before they have mastered the grammatical principles.

Hoemann, Harry, and Shirley Hoemann. *Sign Language Flash Cards: Vol. I*. Bowling Green, Ohio: Bowling Green Press. Contains 500 signs bound in book form, but designed to separate into flash cards.

Hoemann, Harry, Shirley Hoemann, and Rosemarie Lucafo. *Sign Language Flash Cards: Vol. II*. Bowling Green, Ohio: Bowling Green Press. Contains 500 signs bound in book form, but designed to separate into flash cards.

Humphries, Tom, Carol Padden, and Terrence O'Rourke. *A Basic Course in American Sign Language*. 2d ed. Silver Spring, Md.: T.J. Publishers, 1994. This text contains twenty-two lessons plans that present ASL as a second language. Approximately 1,000 signs are included.

Riekehof, Lottie. *The Joy of Signing*. 2d ed. Springfield, Mo: Gospel Publishing House, 1987. A basic text that includes sign origins, practice sentences, and descriptions of handshapes and movements.

Schein, Jerome D., and David A. Stewart. *Language in Motion, Exploring the Nature of Sign*. Washington, D.C.: Gallaudet University Press, 1995. Explores the relationship of ASL to other sign languages in the world. The structure of ASL is discussed as well as the history of sign language.

Shroyer, Edgar. *Signs of the Times*. Washington, D.C.: Gallaudet University Press, 1982. The emphasis of this book is on learning Manually Coded English. Forty-one lessons are included. Unique are the "mind ticklers" that use mnemonics to help readers remember the signs.

Shroyer, Edgar, and Susan Shroyer. *Signs Across America*. Washington, D.C.: Gallaudet University Press, 1984. A look at regional variation in ASL. This book contains sign variations from across the United States for 130 different words. It includes an explanation of why signs may differ from place to place.

Sternberg, Martin. *American Sign Language Dictionary*. New York: Harper and Row, 1981. This dictionary describes more than 3,000 frequently used signs. Each sign is cross-referenced.

Valli, Clayton, and Ceil Lucas. *Linguistics of American Sign Language: An Introduction*. 2d ed. Washington, D.C.: Gallaudet University Press, 1995. The most current information available on the structure of ASL. Course videotape also available.

Materials on Deafness

Batson, Trent, and Eugene Bergman, eds. *Angels and Outcasts: An Anthology of Deaf Characters in Literature*. Washington, D.C.: Gallaudet University Press, 1985. A collection of stories that explores the attitudes and prejudices common to western cultures about deaf people.

Christiansen, John, and Sharon Barnartt. *Deaf President Now! The 1988 Revolution at Gallaudet University*. Washington, D.C.: Gallaudet University Press, 1995. A study of the history-making revolution at Gallaudet in 1988 that resulted in the appointment of the first deaf president of the university.

Freeman, Roger, Clifton Carbin, and Robert Boese. *Can't Your Child Hear?* Baltimore, Md.: University Park Press, Austin, Tex.: PRO-ED, 1981. This reference will help parents and teachers understand issues related to deafness such as communication, education, and rehabilitation. It is an excellent resource for anyone who wants to understand the issues surrounding the education of deaf children.

Gannon, Jack. *Deaf Heritage: A Narrative History of Deaf America*. Silver Spring, Md.: National Association of the Deaf, 1981. This book has samplings of many aspects of deaf culture: deaf humor, deaf artists, schools for the deaf, and deaf athletes. The text is full of photographs and illustrations. Each school for the deaf is profiled.

Jacobs, Leo. *A Deaf Adult Speaks Out*, 3d ed. Washington, D.C.: Gallaudet University Press, 1989. This book is a personal account of what it is like to be deaf. Mr. Jacobs comments on issues important to deaf people, such as total communication, oralism, residential schools, mainstreaming, and more.

Lane, Harlan. *When the Mind Hears*. New York: Vintage Books, 1989. This is a well-written, sensitive account of the history of deaf people and its relationship to the hearing academic community. The story is told from the viewpoint of Laurent Clerc, the first deaf teacher of the deaf in the United States. The oral-manual controversy as it exists today is examined.

Spradley, Thomas, and James Spradley. *Deaf Like Me*. Washington, D.C.: Gallaudet University Press, 1985. This sensitive story tells what it is like for a family to come to terms with deafness. This is an excellent resource for examining attitudes about disabilities.

ADDITIONAL RESOURCES

Organizations

Alexander Graham Bell Association for the Deaf
3417 Volta Place, NW
Washington, DC 20007
(202) 337-5220
A.G. Bell is an organization that promotes the use of auditory/oral skills. This organization sponsors an oral deaf adults group as well as a parents group. Write for the free catalog of materials on deafness.

The National Association of the Deaf
814 Thayer Avenue
Silver Spring, MD 20910
(301) 587-1788
The National Association of the Deaf (NAD) is the oldest consumer
organization of disabled people in the United States. It has more than
20,000 members, and it is the advocate for more than 16 million deaf and
hard of hearing people in the United States. NAD has many services;
among them are a legal defense fund, a communicative skills program, and
a book publishing and sales division. Write or call for a catalog.

National Information Center on Deafness
Gallaudet University
800 Florida Avenue NE
Washington, DC 20002
(202) 651-5051 (voice)
(202) 651-5052 (tty)
The National Information Center on Deafness (NICD) is a centralized
source of information about hearing loss and deafness. NICD collects,
develops, and disseminates up-to-date information on deafness, hearing
loss, organizations, and services for deaf and hard of hearing people. Write
or call for information or a catalog.

Publishers and Suppliers

DawnSign Press
9080 Activity Road
Suite A
San Diego, CA 92126

Deafness Gallery at Gallaudet University
800 Florida Avenue NE
Washington, DC 20002

Gallaudet University Press
800 Florida Avenue NE
Washington, DC 20002

Sign Media, Inc.
4020 Blackburn Lane
Burtonsville, MD 20866

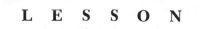

GLOSSARY

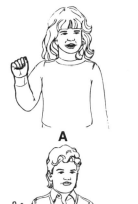

A

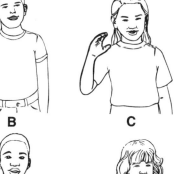

B

C

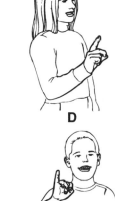

D

E

F

G

H

I

J

K

L

M

N

O

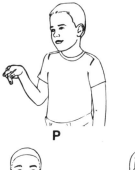

P

Q

R

S

T

U

V

W

X

Y

Z

about

1 handshape both hands, palms in. Circle left index finger with right index finger. (p. 80)

airplane

I LOVE YOU handshape right hand, palm down. Move hand forward and up. (p. 101)

Angela

A handshape right hand. Tap hand against left shoulder. (p. 41)

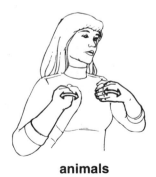

animals

Open B handshape both hands, fingertips on upper chest. Bend hands in and out several times. (p. 85)

afraid

Flat O handshape both hands, palms in. Bring hands in toward chest, opening to 5 handshape. (p. 5)

and

5 handshape right hand, palm in. Move hand to the right, closing to a flat O handshape. (p. 80)

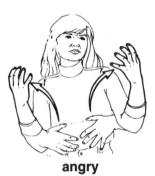

angry

Claw handshape both hands, palms in, fingertips on stomach. Move hands up and out from chest. (p. 5)

any

10 handshape left hand, palm up. Twist hand down. (p. 28)

apple

X handshape right hand. Press knuckle into cheek and twist hand forward. (p. 91)

baby

Open B handshape both hands, palms up. Mime rocking a baby in your arms. (p. 48)

baseball

A handshape both hands. Mime holding a bat and swinging at a ball. (p. 65)

basketball

Claw handshape both hands, palms facing. Mime holding a ball and move hands up twice. (p. 65)

bear

Claw handshape both hands. Hands crossed over chest. Scratch shoulders twice. (p. 85)

best

Open B handshape left hand, palm in, fingertips touching lips. Move hand down and out, ending in 10 handshape. (p. 65)

bicycle

S handshape both hands, palms down. Move hands in a peddling motion. (p. 101)

big

Bent L handshape both hands, palms facing. Move hands apart. (p. 53)

Billy

B handshape right hand, thumb touching chest. (p. 41)

blue

B handshape right hand, palm in. Twist hand back and forth. (p. 96)

book

Open B handshape both hands. Place palms together and mime opening a book. (p. 111)

brother

A handshape right hand, thumb on forehead; L handshape left hand, palm right. Move right hand down on top of left hand, opening to L handshape. (p. 48)

black

1 handshape right hand, palm down. Slide index finger across forehead. (p. 96)

boat

Open B handshape both hands, little fingers touching. Move hands forward. (p. 101)

boys

Flat O handshape right hand, palm down. Place hand on forehead and open and close hand several times. (p. 111)

brown

B handshape right hand, index finger on cheek. Move hand down along cheek. (p. 96)

but

1 handshape, both hands, palms down, index fingers crossed. Move hands apart. (p. 80)

can

S handshape both hands, palms out. Move hands down once. (pp. 28, 80)

car

S handshape both hands, palms in. Mime driving a car. (p. 101)

carrot

S handshape right hand at side of mouth. Twist hand forward. (p. 91)

cat

F handshape both hands touching sides of mouth. Move hands out to mimic cat whiskers. (p. 85)

celebrate

A handshape both hands. Make circles in the air several times. (p. 75)

cereal

Open B handshape both hands, palms up. Place right hand inside left palm, then move up to lips twice. (p. 91)

Christmas

C handshape right hand, palm left; B handshape left hand, arm extended, palm down. Place right elbow on back of left hand, and right thumb on left elbow. Move right hand up. (p. 75)

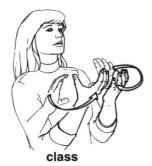

class

C handshape both hands, palms in, thumbs almost touching. Move hands apart and around, ending with little fingers touching. (p. 96)

Clerc

H handshape left hand, thumb extended, fingertips at side of mouth. Brush fingers against cheek twice. (p. 6)

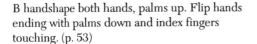

closed

B handshape both hands, palms up. Flip hands ending with palms down and index fingers touching. (p. 53)

cold

A handshape both hands, palms facing. Move hands slightly in a shivering motion. (p. 53)

color

Open B handshape right hand, palm up; 1 handshape left hand, palm down. Slide left index finger across right palm several times. (p. 96)

commitment

S handshape right hand, thumb side up; 1 handshape left hand, touching chin. Bring left hand down and change to open B handshape, covering right S. (p. 5)

communicate

C handshape both hands, palms facing. Move hands alternately back and forth from mouth. (p. 111)

congratulations

Open B handshape both hands, palms facing. Clap hands together 2 or 3 times. (p. 1)

cookie

Open B handshape left hand, palm up; claw handshape right hand, palm down. Place right claw in left palm and twist several times. (p. 91)

cow

Y handshape right hand, thumb on right temple. Twist hand forward once. (p. 85)

day

B handshape left hand, arm extended, palm down; 1 handshape right hand. Rest right elbow on back of left hand and move right hand down to left elbow. (p. 70)

Derrick

D handshape right hand. Tap hand against left shoulder. (p. 41)

cooperate

F handshape both hands, palms facing. Hook thumbs and index fingers together and move counterclockwise in a circle. (p. 43)

crayon

Open B handshape left hand, palm up; 1 handshape right hand, palm down. Slide right index finger across left palm several times. (p. 96)

deaf

1 handshape left hand. Touch ear with index finger, then move it down to chin. (p. 7, 33)

different

D handshape both hands, palms down. Cross index fingers in front of body, then pull hands apart. (p. 53)

do

C handshape both hands, palms down. Move hands side to side 2 or 3 times. (p. 28, 60)

do

Fingerspell D-O. (p. 28)

dog

Open B handshape right hand, arm down. Tap right palm against right leg twice. (p. 85)

don't

Open B handshape both hands palms down, arms crossed in front of body. Draw hands apart. (p. 80)

down

1 handshape right hand, palm down. Point down with index finger. (p. 53)

drink

C handshape right hand. Place thumb near mouth and twist hand up as if drinking from a glass. (p. 91)

each

10 handshape both hands, knuckles touching. Move right hand down. (p. 70)

eat

Flat O handshape right hand. Bring hand up to lip. (p. 60)

elephant

B handshape right hand, palm down. Move hand down from nose and outline an elephant's trunk. (p. 85)

family

F handshape both hands, thumbs and index fingers touching. Move hands out and around until little fingers touch. (p. 48)

farm

5 handshape right hand. Place thumb on left side of chin, then move it across to right side of chin. (p. 85)

favorite

5 handshape right hand, palm in. Touch chin with middle finger. (p. 111)

fall

V handshape right hand, held upside down. Flip hand out and down, ending with palm up. (p. 60)

far

A handshape both hands, thumbs up. Place right hand on top of left and move right hand out and up. (p. 53)

father

5 handshape right hand. Place thumb on forehead. (p. 48)

fine

5 handshape right hand, thumb touching chest. Move hand forward slightly. (p. 33)

finish

5 handshape both hands, palms in. Turn hands out and away from body, ending with palms down. (p. 43)

fireworks

S handshape both hands, palms out. Alternate flicking open hands to illustrate fireworks exploding. (p. 75)

first

10 handshape left hand, thumb up, palm right; 1 handshape right hand, palm left. Bring right index finger back to meet left thumb. (p. 53)

fish

Open B handshape both hands; right hand palm left, left hand palm right. Touch heel of right hand with left fingertips. Move hands forward while wiggling right hand. (p. 85)

football

5 handshape both hands, palms in. Mesh fingers together two times. (p. 65)

for

1 handshape left hand, index finger touching forehead. Twist hand out. (p. 101)

Franco

F handshape right hand. Move hand side to side slightly. (p. 41)

Friday

F handshape right hand palm in. Move hand in small circle. (p. 70)

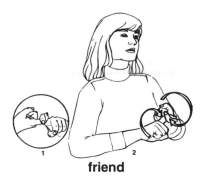

friend

X handshape both hands, right palm up, left palm down. Hook index fingers together, then reverse hand positions. (p. 33)

fun

H handshape both hands, left palm down. Put right H on nose and then on back of left H. (p. 111)

Gallaudet

G handshape left hand, thumb near left eye. Move hand out, closing thumb and index finger together. (p. 6)

girls

10 handshape right hand. Place thumb on cheek and move it down to the chin. (p. 111)

go

1 handshape both hands, palms out. Move hands forward and down. (p. 33)

gold

5 handshape right hand, index finger touching right ear. Move hand down in a wiggling motion. (p. 106)

grandfather

5 handshape right hand, thumb touching forehead. Move hand out in two short movements. (p. 48)

grandmother

5 handshape right hand, thumb touching chin. Move hand forward in two motions. (p. 48)

green

G handshape right hand, palm in. Twist hand back and forth. (p. 96)

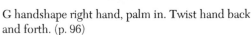

hamburger

C handshape both hands. Clasp hands together, then reverse position and clasp hands again. (p. 91)

Hanukkah

4 handshape both hands palms out, index fingers close together. Move hands out and up in the shape of a menorah. (p. 75)

have

Open B handshape both hands. Move hands in to touch chest. (p. 80)

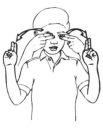

Halloween

B handshape both hands, palms in, hands over eyes. Turn hands out and away from face, ending with palms out. (p. 75)

hand

5 handshape left hand, palm out; 1 handshape right hand, palm in. Point to left hand with right index finger. (p. 18)

happy

Open B handshape left hand, palm in. Brush hand against chest twice. (p. 75)

helicopter

1 handshape left hand, palm right; 5 handshape right hand, palm down. Place right palm on left index finger and shake fingers. (p. 101)

hello

B handshape right hand, touching temple. Move hand out. (p. 33)

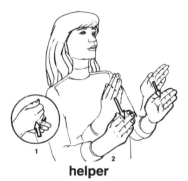

helper

Open B handshape left hand, palm up; A handshape right hand, thumb up. Place right hand in left palm and raise both hands. Change to open B handshape both hands, palms facing. Move hands down. (p. 43)

holiday

5 handshape both hands, palms facing, thumbs extended. Tap thumbs under shoulders twice. (p. 75)

hot

Claw handshape right hand, covering mouth. Turn hand out and down. (p. 53)

help

Open B handshape left hand, palm up; 10 handshape right hand. Place right hand in left palm and move both hands up. (p. 43)

hockey

Open B handshape left hand, palm up; X handshape right hand, palm up. Move right X hand back and forth across left palm. (p. 65)

horse

H handshape both hands, thumbs extended, palms out. Place thumbs on temple and bend fingers twice. (p. 85)

how

C handshape both hands, palms down, back of fingers together. Turn hands out, ending with palms up. (p. 28)

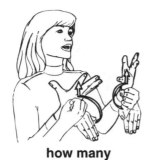

how many

Open B handshape both hands, palms down. Turn hands up into O handshape and flick fingers open. (p. 48)

I

1 handshape right hand, index finger on chest. (p. 48, 80)

I love you

Little finger, index finger, and thumb extended, palm out. (p. 111)

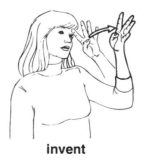

invent

4 handshape left hand, index finger touching forehead. Move hand up and out. (p. 38)

hungry

Claw handshape left hand, palm in. Place hand on chest and move it down. (p. 91)

ice cream

S handshape right hand between mouth and chin. Mime licking an ice cream cone. (p. 91)

independence

I handshape both hands palms in, little fingers touching. Move hands out and twist, ending with palms out. (p. 75)

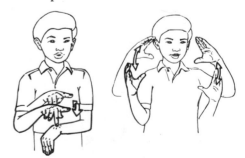

jack-o-lantern

Bent B handshape left hand, palm down; P handshape right hand, palm down, above left hand. Flick thumb and middle finger of right hand on back of left hand twice. Then C handshape both hands, palms facing. Alternately move hands up and down along sides of face. (p. 75)

jump

Open B handshape left hand, palm up; V handshape right hand, fingers pointing down. Place tips of inverted V in left palm. Pull up to mime jumping, ending with bent V handshape. (p. 60)

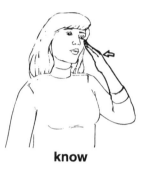

know

Open B handshape left hand. Touch fingertips to temple. (p. 53)

last

I handshape both hands, palms facing. Bring right I down past left I, touching briefly. (p. 53)

learn

Open B handshape left hand, palm up; 4 handshape right hand, palm down. Place right fingertips in left palm, then move right hand up to forehead, ending with flat O handshape. (p. 111)

keep

K handshape both hands, right hand on top of left. Tap right hand on left twice. (p. 106)

land

5 handshape both hands, palms down. Move hands out in a semicircle. (p. 101)

Laura

L handshape right hand, thumb touching right side of mouth. (p. 39)

like

5 handshape left hand, middle finger and thumb on chest. Draw hand out, closing thumb and middle finger together. (p. 65)

line up

4 handshape both hands, left in front of right, fingers touching. Draw hands apart to form an imaginary line of people. (p. 43)

lion

Claw handshape right hand. Place hand over forehead, then move it back to outline a mane. (p. 85)

live

L handshape both hands, index fingers pointing in. Move hands up from waist. (p. 33)

love

S handshape both hands. Cross hands over chest. (p. 48)

meet

L handshape both hands, palms facing. Bring hands together. (p. 33, 106)

menorah

4 handshape both hands, palms out, index fingers close together. Move hands in the shape of a menorah. (p. 75)

milk

5 handshape right hand, palm in. Squeeze hand into S handshape twice. (p. 91)

Monday

M handshape right hand, palm in. Move hand in small circle. (p. 70)

mother

5 handshape right hand. Touch thumb to chin several times. (p. 48)

my

Open B handshape right hand, palm on chest. (p. 33)

near

Open B handshape both hands, palms facing chest, left hand in front of right. Move right hand to left hand, until hands almost touch. (p. 53)

off

Open B handshape both hands, right hand on top of left. Move right hand up off of left. (p. 53)

motorcycle

S handshape both hands, palms down. Mime holding the handlebars of a motorcycle, twisting hands up and down. (p. 101)

name

H handshape both hands. Place middle finger of right H across index finger of left H and tap twice. (p. 33)

new

Open B handshape both hands, palms up. Scoop right hand inward across left palm. (p. 106)

old

S handshape right hand. Pull hand down from chin to mimic a beard. (p. 33)

Olympics

F handshape both hands. Interlock thumbs and index fingers. Move hands across chest, reversing hands and interlocking fingers. (p. 65)

on

Open B handshape both hands, palms down. Place right palm on back of left hand. (p. 53)

one

1 handshape right hand, palm out. (p. 4, 108)

open

B handshape both hands, palms down, index fingers touching. Move hands out ending with palms up. (p. 53)

opposites

1 handshape both hands, palms in, index fingers touching. Move hands apart. (p. 53)

orange

Claw handshape right hand, palm left. Place hand at mouth and squeeze into S handshape several times. (p. 96)

other

10 handshape right hand, palm down. Move hand up and over so palm faces up. (p. 106)

our

Open B handshape left hand, thumb on left shoulder. Extend hand out and around to right shoulder. (p. 96)

Peggy

P handshape right hand. Tap hand against left shoulder. (p. 42)

people

P handshape both hands. Move hands alternately in circular motion away from body. (p. 48)

perseverance

10 handshape both hands, palms down, thumbs touching. Move hands forward. (p. 5)

pets

Open B handshape both hands, palms down. Brush fingertips of right hand across back of left hand twice. (p. 85)

pig

B handshape right hand, palm down. Place hand under chin and bend fingers down. (p. 85)

pipe

Y handshape left hand. Bring thumb to left side of mouth. (p. 2)

pizza

P handshape right hand, palm out. Draw a Z in the air. (p. 91)

play

Y handshape both hands. Twist hands back and forth simultaneously. (p. 60)

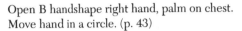

please

Open B handshape right hand, palm on chest.
Move hand in a circle. (p. 43)

popcorn

S handshape both hands, palms in, knuckles up.
Flick index fingers up alternately. (p. 91)

purple

P handshape right hand. Twist hand back and
forth. (p. 96)

putting it all together

4 handshape both hands, palms in. Bring hands
together to mesh fingers. (p. 80)

questions

1 handshape left hand. Draw question mark in the
air with left index finger. (p. 28)

rabbit

H handshape both hands, right hand on top of left.
Wiggle H hands to mimic rabbit ears. (p. 85)

rainbow

4 handshape left hand, palm down. Arch hand up
and over to outline a rainbow. (p. 96)

read

Open B handshape left hand, V handshape right
hand; palms facing. Move right V down across left
palm. (p. 60)

red

1 handshape right hand, palm in, fingertip on mouth. Move hand down across lips. (p. 96)

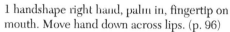

restroom

R handshape right hand, palm down. Move hand from left to right. (p. 43)

rocket

Open B handshape left hand, palm right; R handshape right hand, palm left. Place right R in left palm and move hand up. (p. 101)

Sam

S handshape right hand. Tap hand against left shoulder. (p. 42)

rest

Open B handshape both hands. Cross hands over chest. (p. 60)

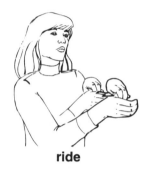

ride

Bent V handshape left hand, C handshape right hand. Hook bent V into right thumb and move hands forward. (p. 101)

run

L handshape both hands. Hook left index finger into right thumb and move hands forward wiggling index fingers and thumbs. (p. 60)

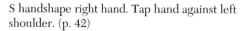

same

Y handshape right hand, palm down. Move hand side to side. (p. 53, 106)

sandwich

Open B handshape both hands, palms touching. Move hands to mouth twice so fingertips touch lips. (p. 91)

school

5 handshape both hands, right palm down, left palm up. Clap hands together twice. (p. 33)

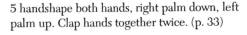

shoes

S handshape both hands; palms down. Bring hands together twice. (p. 2)

show

Open B handshape left hand, palm right; 1 handshape right hand, palm left. Place right index finger in left palm and move both hands forward. (p. 111)

Saturday

S handshape right hand palm in. Move hand in a small circle. (p. 70)

sheep

Left arm pointing down, V handshape right hand. Move right V up left arm making a scissors motion twice. (p. 85)

short

Open B handshape right hand, fingers bent, palm down. Lower hand to indicate height. (p. 53)

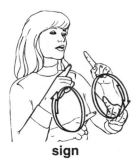

sign

1 handshape both hands, palms out. Move hands alternately in circular motion in toward body. (p. 7)

silver

S handshape right hand, thumb against right ear.
Move hand down in a wiggling motion. (p. 106)

sit down

H handshape both hands, palms down, right hand
above left. Bring right H down to touch left H.
(p. 43)

sleep

5 handshape right hand, palm in. Place hand in front of
face and move out, closing to a flat O handshape. (p. 60)

snake

Bent V handshape right hand at side of mouth.
Move hand out in circular motion. (p. 85)

sister

10 handshape right hand, thumb on cheek; L
handshape left hand, palm right. Move right hand down
on top of left hand, changing to L handshape. (p. 48)

skateboard

Open B handshape both hands, palms down; right
hand in front of left. Move hands forward, sliding
side to side. (p. 65)

small

Open B handshape both hands, palms facing.
Bring hands toward each other. (p. 53)

soccer

Open B handshape both hands, left palm down,
right palm left. Place right hand under left and
bring up to left palm twice. (p. 65)

some

Open B handshape, both hands. Draw left hand across right palm. (p. 38)

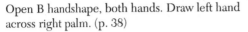

special

1 handshape left hand, palm in. Grasp left index finger with right thumb and index finger and pull up. (p. 70)

sport

A handshape both hands, palms facing. Move hands alternately back and forth. (p. 65)

Sunday

Open B handshape both hands, palms out. Move hands in circular motion. (p. 70)

song

Open B handshape both hands, palms in, right hand in back of left. Move right hand up and back in an arc. (p. 106)

spell

5 handshape left hand, palm down. Move hand from right to left while wiggling fingers. (p. 18)

stop

Open B handshape both hands, left hand palm up, right hand palm left. Bring little finger side of right hand down on left palm. (p. 43)

sweetheart

10 handshape both hands, knuckles touching, near heart. Bend and straighten thumbs several times. (p. 75)

talk

1 handshape both hands, palms facing. Move hands alternately back and forth from lips. (p. 111)

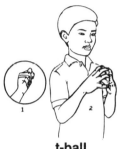

t-ball

T handshape right hand; then claw handshape both hands, palms facing. Touch fingertips together to form an imaginary ball. (p. 65)

team

T handshape both hands, palms out, index fingers touching. Move hands apart and around to front, ending with little fingers touching. (p. 65)

thank you

Open B handshape right hand, palm up. Touch chin with fingertips and move hand out. (p. 43)

tall

Open B handshape right hand, fingers bent, palm down. Raise hand to indicate height. (p. 53)

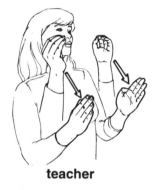

teacher

O handshape both hands. Move hands down into open B handshape. (p. 43)

tennis

A handshape right hand, Mime hitting a ball with a racket. (p. 65)

Thanksgiving

Open B handshape both hands, palms in, fingertips at chin. Move hands out and down in two short movements. (p. 75)

things

Open B handshape left hand, palm up. Bounce hand to the left in two movements. (p. 60)

this

Open B handshape left hand, palm up; 1 handshape right hand, palm down. Touch middle of left palm with right index finger. (p. 80)

thrilling

5 handshape both hands, middle fingers bent, touching chest. Move hands up and out off of chest. (p. 5)

Thursday

T handshape right hand, palm out. Change to H handshape. (p. 70)

ticket

B handshape left hand palm in; bent V handshape right hand. Slide right V onto palm of left hand. (p. 101)

time

S handshape right hand, palm down; 1 handshape left hand, palm down. Point to right wrist with left index finger. (p. 91)

to

1 handshape both hands. Move left index finger to touch right index finger. (p. 101)

to be

1 handshape left hand, index finger touching chin. Move hand forward. (p. 43)

to do

Claw handshape both hands. Move hands side to side. (p. 60)

tree

5 handshape right hand, palm in; open B handshape left hand, arm extended, palm down. Place right elbow on back of left hand and twist right hand back and forth. (p. 75)

Tuesday

T handshape right hand. Move hand in small circle. (p. 70)

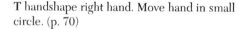

up

1 handshape right hand, palm out. Point up with index finger. (p. 53)

train

H handshape both hands, palms down. Move right H back and forth across left H. (p. 101)

trip

Bent V handshape right hand, palm out. Move hand forward and up. (p. 101)

turkey

G handshape right hand, palm left, side of index finger at chin. Move hand down to chest. (p. 75)

Valentine's Day

5 handshape both hands, palms in. Draw outline of heart with middle fingers of both hands. (p. 75)

very

V handshape both hands, fingertips touching.
Move hands apart. (p. 2)

wait

5 handshape both hands, palms up. Hold hands
out in front of body with left hand slightly in front.
Wiggle fingers. (p. 43)

walk

Open B handshape both hands, palms down.
Mime walking with hands several times. (p. 60)

want

Claw handshape both hands, palms up. Bring
hands in toward body and bend fingers. (p. 33)

we

1 handshape left hand. Touch left shoulder with
index finger, then move to right shoulder. (p. 33)

Wednesday

W handshape right hand, palm in. Move hand in
small circle. (p. 70)

week

Open B handshape left hand, palm up; 1 handshape
right hand, palm down. Move right hand across left
palm from heel to fingertips. (p. 70)

what

Open B handshape left hand; 1 handshape right
hand. Draw right index finger across left palm
from top to bottom. (p. 28)

what?

5 handshape both hands, palms up. Move hands slightly together and apart several times. (p. 5)

What's up?

5 handshape both hands, middle fingers bent, touching chest. Move hands up and out with a questioning look on face. (p. 28)

where

1 handshape right hand. Shake hand side to side with a questioning look on face. (p. 28)

white

5 handshape right hand, fingertips on chest. Move hand out and close fingers to form flat O handshape. (p. 96)

What are you doing?

G handshape both hands, palms up. Open and close thumbs and index fingers several times with a questioning look on face. (p. 28)

when

1 handshape both hands, index fingers touching. Move right finger out and around in a circle. (p. 28)

which

10 handshape both hands, thumbs up, palms in. Move hands alternately up and down. (p. 80)

who

1 handshape right hand. Circle the mouth. (p. 28)

why

5 handshape right hand, middle finger touching right temple. Move hand down and out into Y handshape. (p. 28)

will

Open B handshape right hand, palm left near face. Move hand out and forward. (p. 80)

with

A handshape both hands, palms facing. Bring hands together. (p. 18)

words

G handshape left hand, 1 handshape right hand, palms facing. Place left G on right index finger. (p. 18)

write

Flat O handshape right hand; open B handshape left hand. Mime writing in left palm with thumb and index finger of right hand holding an imaginary pen. (p. 60)

yellow

Y handshape right hand, palm out. Twist hand back and forth. (p. 96)

you

1 handshape left hand, index finger pointing out. (p. 28)

your

Open B handshape right hand, palm out. Move hand out toward person you are speaking to. (p. 33)